AFTER-SCHOOL AND PARENT EDUCATION PROGRAMS FOR AT-RISK YOUTH AND THEIR FAMILIES

About the Author

Tommie Morton-Young is a native of Nashville, Tennessee where she presently resides. She received her early education in the public schools of the city and graduated cum laude from Tennessee State University. She holds the M.A. degree from Peabody/Vanderbilt University and the Ph.D. degree from Duke University.

She formerly served as Professor of Education and Director of Instructional Services at North Carolina Agricultural & Technical State University, and is Adjunct Professor of English at Tennessee State University. She is author of several published articles, poems, and books including *Afro American Genealogy Sourcebook* and *Oral Histories of Four Former All-Black Public Schools in Two North Carolina Counties.*

A member of Phi Kappa Phi Honor Society and Beta Phi Mu Scholastic Fraternity, she is listed in *Who's Who* including *Who's Who of American Women, Who's Who in Colleges and Universities,* and *Who's Who of Business and Professional Women.*

AFTER-SCHOOL AND PARENT EDUCATION PROGRAMS FOR AT-RISK YOUTH AND THEIR FAMILIES

A Guide to Organizing and Operating
a Community-Based Center for Basic
Educational Skills Reinforcement,
Homework Assistance, Cultural Enrichment,
and a Parent Involvement Focus

By

TOMMIE MORTON-YOUNG

Adjunct Professor
Tennessee State University
Nashville, Tennessee

C H A R L E S   C   T H O M A S • P U B L I S H E R
Springfield • Illinois • U.S.A.

Published and Distributed Throughout the World by

CHARLES C THOMAS • PUBLISHER
2600 South First Street
Springfield, Illinois 62794-9265

© *1995 by* CHARLES C THOMAS • PUBLISHER
ISBN 0-398-05961-6   (cloth)
ISBN 0-398-05962-4   (paper)
Library of Congress Catalog Card Number: 94-38716

With **THOMAS BOOKS** *careful attention is given to all details of manufacturing
and design. It is the Publisher's desire to present books that are satisfactory as to their
physical qualities and artistic possibilities and appropriate for their particular use.*
THOMAS BOOKS *will be true to those laws of quality that assure a good name
and good will.*

Printed in the United States of America
SC-R-3

Library of Congress Cataloging-in-Publication Data

Morton-Young, Tommie.
    After-school and parent education programs for at-risk youth and
their families : a guide to organizing and operating a community-
based center for basic educational skills reinforcement, homework
assistance, cultural enrichment, and a parent involvement focus / by
Tommie Morton-Young.
        p.   cm.
    Includes bibliographical references and index.
    ISBN 0-398-05961-6 (cloth). — ISBN 0-398-05962-4 (paper)
    1. Basic education—United States.   2. Education—Parent
participation—United States.   3. School-age child care—United
States.   I. Title.
LC1035.6.M67   1995
370.11—dc20   94-38716
                                                       CIP

It takes a whole village to raise a child.
African Proverb

PREFACE

This work is about *after-school* programs that are designed to assist students in completing homework, aid youth in acquiring basic educational and social skills, and their parents in becoming more effective agents in their children's schooling experiences.

The book is intended for use by community organizers, parent/child advocates, parents, teacher education programs and field experience classes, and as a supplementary resource for schools.

The work is divided into four (IV) parts: Part I—Getting Started; Part II—Planning and Implementing the Program; Part III—Parent Programs; and Part IV—Resources Directory.

The premise of this work is that in a changing society, the schools, a place where most children are required to go, are the more likely agencies to close the gaps in the development of youth left by upheavals in the home and fluctuating social experiences. Since schools are increasingly overextended and are limited in what they may do, this need can more readily be met after school by partnerships formed of community groups which develop programs designed to serve children and families in a variety of ways. After-school programs can offer such services as adult mentoring and nurturing, assistance in academic skills efforts, and provision of leadership for parents.

This work is a response to a number of concerns that impact the lives of children, families, and the schools. It is based on program ideas and procedures implemented in university learning laboratories and community-based projects directed by university staffs, local community leaders and the author of this work for more than twenty years.

T.M.Y.

ACKNOWLEDGMENTS

The author of this work acknowledges with appreciation the cooperation of parents, teachers, students, volunteers, faculty and staffs of agencies and institutions that have aided and assisted the various projects and developmental centers and their programs with which the author has been affiliated. Many ideas, activities, and theories discussed in this book evolved from practical experiences in various after-school and learning center projects. The author also acknowledges the financial assistance that various funding agencies have given over the years in support of some of the after-school and parent education programs with which she has been associated.

CONTENTS

AFTER-SCHOOL AND PARENT EDUCATION PROGRAMS FOR AT-RISK YOUTH AND THEIR FAMILIES

Introduction

CHANGING TIMES

American society has experienced dramatic changes in the past forty years. No place are changes more evident than in the family. America has expanded its definition of the family, and the traditional model of nuclear family—father, mother and child or children—has given way to more than one configuration. Families now include relationships of gay and lesbian couples, many of whom have children, unmarried heterosexual couples, step families, and the so-called *skip-generation families* (Seligmann, 1990) in which grandparents raise the children of their children. The phrase *head of family* has been replaced by the term *householder.* Current statistics reveal that more householders are females without a spouse.

Two parents working outside the home is said to be the most dramatic change in the family's changing patterns. As a result, children are often left unsupervised for many hours, particularly during after-school hours. As mothers go to work, young children, often beginning in infancy, are attended by a variety of caretakers. These children are with caretakers during most of their waking hours and may be exposed to differing values transmitted by the caretakers. Some authorities attribute children's attitudes toward authority in the home and the school to be the result of having a variety of authority figure in their lives and upbringing. This raises an alarming question: *Who's taking care of the children?*

Another impact on the time parents have to spend with their children is travel. Many must travel miles to and from work. Transportation time whittles away at the time the parent can spend with the child and adds stress to the lives of both parent and child.

While both the single- and the two-parent family must cope with the challenges of time and distance separating them from their children, the single-parent family often finds family life as being near havoc. Thus, children of single-parent families where the mother is the sole wage earner tend to experience more social and school problems.

Picture the schoolchild of the past. The school day ends, the child goes home where an adult awaits to greet him: mother, grandmother, aunt, uncle, an older sibling. Or, perhaps the child goes next door to the home of a neighbor or relative. The child changes from school clothes to play clothes, has a snack, then sets about doing chores. Where the child lives determines the type of chores. Children in rural areas more often have very specific duties critical to the survival of the family. Upon completing the chores, the child plays until supper time when the family gathers around a table more likely of simple, but nutritious food. The family talks—shares the day's events. After supper, older siblings help the child with schoolwork, or parents are nearby, ready to help or ensure homework is done.

Thus passed the day in the life of the child of the past, who lived in a safe, secure environment surrounded by people who loved and cared for him. In this environment there were regularity, expectations and responsibility, stability, support, and a sense of well-being.

Today, *latchkey* has come to identify those children who come home from school five afternoons a week to find a house void of human presence. The child lets himself into the house to find silence. For him, television is the most available source of images and sound, and the television becomes the companion and sitter. Alone and desirous of quelling the sound of silence, the child is likely to choose the most exciting and provocative program that can be found.

The child of today is less likely to go to a neighbor's house. America's sense of community has changed. Families are far more mobile. Children are less likely to be born in and grow up in the same community. Many do not know their neighbors—neighbors come and go. By the time the child is ten he is likely to have lived in at least two different communities. New communities crop up every day, and housing developments and planned communities often include neighbors who meet only during association meetings or in passing. The absence of the sense of community affects children and families who may drift toward feelings of isolation and alienation. The declining sense of safety causes parents to teach children to avoid strangers, and people are becoming increasingly suspicious and fearful of each other. Assuring that the child is in a safe place while parents are at work is a priority for most working parents. Finding that place is often a challenge.

Technology has altered America's way of life. It has reduced the number of hours and routines required to sustain daily life. Youth have fewer responsibilities and chores to perform in the home. This creates more free time. These hours are often filled with mindless watching of television, playing electronic games, or just *hanging out.* Some parents buy expensive gadgets and devices as a compensation for the time not shared with their children. Many of these devices and toys encourage violence and aggressive behavior.

There is need for parents to find ways to keep their children involved with things that have purpose and meaning and desirable outcomes. There is a need for agencies in the community to help parents in perceiving the kinds of needs that children have.

The layout of America's communities requires automobiles in order to get around. Suburbia is home for millions of families. Parents work and are not available to transport youth to the many sites that their lives demand. Public transportation in middle and smaller-sized communities is often inefficient or lacking. Parents fear for their children walking to places and being on the streets. Therefore, automobiles for youth are more often necessities than luxuries. Yet, automobiles pose problems for youth. Youth can go to places today that would have not been readily accessible in the past. Automobiles can provide a place and an opportunity for a number of behaviors that are negative. Deaths of youths by and in automobiles are seen in painful annual statistics. Speeding, driving under the influence, and careless driving habits are often cited as the causes of youth fatalities.

Many high school youth work after school and require automobiles. Many youth work to pay for their automobiles. As a result, their school-work and health often suffer. Automobiles are a mixed blessing for the young.

Experimentations and abuse of illegal substances, access to firearms and weapons, and unsupervised free time take their toll on youth. Children who are inadequately supervised and/or live in critical neighborhoods have been known to be recruited as *drug runners.* Children who have no safe place to go after school may hang out on street corners, porches and yards of neighbors and may be identified as candidates for drug involvement.

CHILDREN AT RISK

The term *at risk* cannot be precisely defined. For some it has come to mean *disadvantaged* and *culturally deprived.* Both of the latter terms tend to be even more imprecise. While many after-school, cultural and educational enrichment programs are addressed to at-risk populations, the fact of the matter is that at-risk populations include a far broader spectrum of society. The Council of Chief State School Officers (1987) identified sixty-seven behaviors that placed youth at risk. Framier and Gansneder (1989) note forty-five factors that place youth at risk, including: underachievement, retention in grade, discipline problems, dropping out of school, low parental support, physical problems, use and abuse of drugs and alcohol, and contemplation of suicide.

At-risk children also include those who are emotionally, psychologically and physically abused: children who are sexually abused, children who *grow up* before their time, children who are in economically depressed homes and communities, and children who are deemed less valuable in society. Thus, *at risk* seems to identify groups of children who are facing academic, social, or personal problems so severe or traumatic that their futures are in jeopardy.

Children who come from environments that are disruptive and disorganized and where there is little source of authority or guidance from mature and stable adults are likely to manifest behavioral and discipline problems. These youth are likely to clash with school routines and challenge school personnel and authorities. These children are likely candidates for internal and external suspensions. They often fall behind in classwork, become school dropouts and continuing social problems. Children who feel rootless or caught in conflict at home find it difficult to pay attention at school and begin to feel lost.

Children who are abused in their home environments are even more at risk for dropping out of school, long-term emotional and psychological problems, and failure in adult life. Child abuse includes both physical and mental abuse. Physical abuse includes outbursts of striking and hitting of children, excessive physical discipline, sexual molestation, and neglect (medical, educational, and personal care). Ridicule and persistent criticisms, unrealistic expectations, and instances where parents ignore their children and provide little emotional support and interaction are examples of mental abuse.

Children who live in home environments where a stream of loosely related persons come and go have been found to be abused by relatives and acquaintances. Reports from social services agencies across the nation indicate that children are more often abused by their mothers or by some male in the home—the father and more often the mother's boyfriend or live-in companion. This person may resent the presence of the child of another male. The changing and broader definition or network of today's family with its declining cohesiveness finds children more and more vulnerable in the place they call home — a place where they should be able to find refuge.

Growing numbers of youth are becoming sexually active at an earlier age. Child development specialists note that these youth, despite their outward appearances of sophistication and maturity, are naive about procreation. Many of the girls become pregnant and few will continue on to complete high school. Far too many end up on public assistance and begin a cycle of dependency from one generation to another, thus creating and perpetuating *at-risk families.*

Another group of children that is at risk is that of children who live out their youth in a society where they are perceived to be of *less value* by the dominant group. Children who sense that they are deemed less worthy than their counterparts of another racial or social class group are likely to perform poorly in school and eventually drop out. Discipline problems and low achievement are common traits of these individuals. These youth may exhibit yet another behavior that stems from the way in which they see themselves reflected in the *eyes* of others: *the mirror image.*

One school of thought has it that Native Americans, Mexican Americans, and African Americans have experienced so many generations of systematic economic discrimination that it has transformed them into an underclass. It is said that the children of these groups share a fatalistic perspective since it seems to them that no amount of work leads to a better job or a better life (Nieto, 1992). This perspective impacts children's view of school and the value they attach to the experience.

Educational practices are also cited as placing children at risk. Wasserman (1970) found that in practice there is the tendency for schools to label all students from poverty (and some ethnic/racial) groups as having learning problems, as not being interested in school, and as likely not to succeed in school.

Hollingshead (1949) found that schools, through a variety of means, give support to differences in treatment based on social class. Ballentine (1983) provides evidence that race is a factor in the separation of students into academic tracks. Children of upper classes are generally placed in college preparatory classes that are stimulating and motivating. Lower class or minority racial/ethnic children are more often placed in general or vocational tracks. Teaching methods tend to follow these tracks. The motivating and stimulating instruction and resources are presented in the classes with the upper-class enrollment, and the limited, less interesting teachers, methods, and resources are assigned to the children of the lower classes.

Giroux (1983) presents an interesting point of view called the *resistance theory*. Giroux argues that schools replicate the social class structure with students being moulded for their place in society. He contends that some students *resist* the efforts of teachers to *mould* them; that these students create their own peer culture that is anti-school. This anti-school culture is disruptive, creates continuing discipline problems, and its practitioners seem determined to fail at school. The very culture rejects hope for upward mobility through school and school values.

Children who are from racial and socioeconomic groups that have been labeled and stereotyped tend to behave in the manner expected. Students who are expected to do well tend to do well; if expected to do poorly, they tend to do poorly. Merton (1948) says children perform in ways teachers expect. This is called the *self-fulfilling prophesy*. Children are vulnerable to many pitfalls in social and academic experiences in life. Some children seem fated by society to be nudged toward at-riskness and must be helped in many ways and through many means in order to circumvent and manage the pitfalls that plague their young existences. Help, undoubtedly, must come from redirected goals and approaches within the school as well as discerning agencies and institutions beyond the school. One way of helping these at-risk young people is to establish after-school programs.

AFTER-SCHOOL PROGRAMS

After-school programs are academic, social, or recreational services offered by public or private agencies to youth in the hours immediately following school. These academic-oriented programs attempt to narrow the gap in the rate of school success among the more affluent and less privileged children; aid youth in developing positive views of themselves, school and society; provide a safe place for children when parents are not available; and assist parents and children in dealing with the social and emotional challenges they face as a result of a changing society and altering family roles.

After-school programs come in various forms and are sponsored by various entities. Commercial programs provide services for profit. Many of these programs are associated with day-care centers and may accept siblings of the younger children who are enrolled, as well as other children. Some of these agencies offer tutoring while others are largely a safe place with custodial care and/or play. Still other nationally recognized commercial after-school centers or programs are designed exclusively for the purpose of offering educational exercises that reinforce the child's school curriculum. The latter programs are often addressed to more affluent families that can provide their children with enrichment experiences throughout the year in such activities as summer camps and *Saturday academies.*

Schools are increasingly called upon to do more and more things in the lives of children. Therefore, children who need and desire special and specific assistance and resources to keep up, catch up, or move ahead get lost in the system. Families who can pay for their children to have tutors or participate in enrichment programs do so; those who cannot pay are left out and are allowed to drift. More programs are needed to meet the multiple needs of youth today—some needs stemming from home and community environments, some from school experience and the ways children are dealt with in them.

More and more civic and social organizations are electing after-school programs as their major service projects. Some organizations operate the after-school services directly. Others choose to support programs through gifts of money and volunteer time. Such organizations as the National Black Child Development Institute, Inc., the Salvation Army's Boys and Girls Club, the Young Men's and Women's Christian Association (YMCA and YWCA), the National Association for the Advancement of Colored People (NAACP), fraternal orders and social fraternities and sororities are among the groups offering *after-school* programs. Local neighborhood clubs and family literacy organizations such as Motheread are focusing more and more on the needs of youth in the schooling process and are making efforts to ensure that youth *stay in school* and *succeed in school.*

Activities of these organizations include the BCDI's **Each One, Reach One,** a program that stresses self-pride and the acquisition of basic learning skills. The **Each One, Reach One** is a major effort to recruit, train and utilize volunteers in tutoring and service to youth. The Salvation Army's Boys and Girls Clubs in many American cities include the **Smart Moves, Junior Frontier,** and **Junior Army** programs. These programs place emphasis on developing positive attitudes and demonstrating positive behavior including leadership development training. The

YMCA's and YWCA's programs vary from city to city. In some cities such as Nashville, Tennessee, programs are sponsored for children during the hours before and after school. Emphasis is placed on nutrition, self-development, and academics. In some cases the programs also work with parents of the children.

The NAACP has a unit called the Youth Service Corps. Through this structure a number of activities are designed to aid youth in positive social as well as intellectual growth. The **Back to School—Stay in School** focus is implemented in different ways in different communities with after-school programs with tutoring and academic counseling in many cases. Some parent education programs are associated with this structure.

Family literacy programs are doing much in the way of aiding children and families in becoming more proficient in reading and understanding social dynamics as well as academic subjects and information. **Motheread,** with headquarters in North Carolina, is a unique program that works with women who are incarcerated in prison through bringing mother and child together for reading sessions and activities. The Motheread concept has been adopted by community programs that are not related to mothers who are in prison.

Project Uplift in North Carolina utilizes the Motheread approach in its work with low-income families. In Nashville, Tennessee, the Neighborhood Education Project notes, *Parents and grandparents learn to read with their children at the NEP Family Reading Clubs.* These clubs focus on reading and mathematics, and through the *NEP NEWS* students have the opportunity to publish their writings. The Child Advocacy/Parent Education (CA/PE) model for after-school services with a parent education component has been demonstrated in Durham and Greensboro, North Carolina since 1971 under the direction of this author. The CA/PE concept uses the *ripple* approach, with parents of children in the after-school program enrolling and participating in the Parent Practica where they make a pledge to share all materials and learnings with at least *one* other parent not in the program.

Some religious denominations and local churches include after-school services as part of the church's outreach ministry. Just as Sunday school in England began to provide young, working, economically depressed children with an opportunity to learn to read (Webb, Metha, & Jordan, 1992), the modern church has an equally compelling opportunity to reach children with varying needs today.

One form of *after-school* program is the *extended school* concept. Extended school is offered by a school district and may be supervised and managed within the district's organizational structure or contracted to another agency. Extended school programs are being suggested as a standard part of the budget and curriculum services of some school districts. It has been suggested by some educators that state-financed plans for extended school be offered and linked to the Federal Chapter I guidelines (Boyer, 1987). Certificates would be offered to poor families to be redeemed at a preschool, after-school, or summer school of their choice. Where parents could afford the fees, families would be charged. Several states have programs that set precedents in this area. They include New Jersey, Pennsylvania, South Carolina and Tennessee. School districts not wishing to include the enrichment programs as part of their internal structure can contract the program to a youth club, civic or education group, a library or a local college.

The *after-school* program concept fostered by this writing differs from the extended school idea as noted above in several ways: the after-school program is a community-based program; it is organized, implemented, and supported by cooperative efforts of two or more private agencies or organizations; the program accepts but does not depend on public funds; it draws on a pool of parent and community volunteers for planning and implementation, and it encourages **self-help;** it creates and fosters a climate and an environment that reflect a quasi-home atmosphere, and it works with parents at a level that may be prohibited in the public school setting.

Most any reputable community group with positive goals and purposes, whether already organized or considering a community-based organization for the purpose of establishing an after-school program, can develop and offer a successful service. A variety of after-school programs can and do exist. After-school programs target children under a variety of labels, and given conditions that define the *at risk* in our present society, there are far more children than may be expected who would profit from the after-school experiences.

WHAT IS AN AFTER-SCHOOL PROGRAM?

An after-school program, in the context of this writing, is a service to children and their parents that may provide the following:

1. A safe place for a child to be during the hours of 2:30 p.m.–5:30 or 6:00 p.m., Monday–Friday.
2. Academic enrichment activities focusing on basic learning skills and techniques in how to learn, home work assistance, and use of tools of learning.
3. Cultural enrichment activities that help the child to better understand and appreciate his cultural origins and himself as a part of his heritage and thus build self-esteem.
4. Social interaction with peers, older adults, and volunteers who provide mentoring and one-on-one tutoring experiences.
5. Parent education that includes seminars on issues of concern to parents, counseling and advice on family matters, and directions and suggestions on how parents and parent surrogates can participate in the child's school growth.

REFERENCES

Baker, N. (1986, March). Rush to learning (Horizon/Sunshine) after-school schemes in Great Britain. *Times Educational Supplement, 3638,21.*

Ballentine, J. (1983). *The sociology of education.* Englewood Cliffs, NJ: Prentice-Hall.

Bennett, K., & LeCompte, M. D. (1990). *How schools work: A sociological analysis of education.* NY: Longmans.

Bergin, A. D. et al. (1992, September). An after-school intervention program for educationally disadvantaged young children (Hilltop Emergency Literacy Program— HELP). *Urban Review, 24,* 203, 17.

Boyer, E. L. (1987, March). Early schooling and the nation's future. *Educational Leadership,* 4–6.

Bronfenbrenner, U. (1986, March). Alienation and the four worlds of childhood. *Phi Delta Kappan,* 430, 36.

Burns, C., Jr. (1992, February). Meeting the academic needs of children after-school. *NAASP Bulletin, 76,* 120–22.

Campbell, L. P., & Flaker, A. E. (1985, May). Latchkey children—What is the answer? *Clearing House, 58,* 381–83.

Comer, James P. (1986, January). Is parenting essential to good teaching? *NEA Today,* 34–40.

Cose, E. (1993, August). Protecting the child. Government programs and black self-help efforts are only part of the solution. What's needed is a change in society itself. *Newsweek,* 28–29.

Council of Chief State School Officers. (1987). *Characteristics of at-risk students.* Washington, D.C.: The Council.

Davis, V. (1988, October). After-school fun (great after school programs). *School Library Journal, 35,* 48.

Drucker, R. F. (1987). How schools must change. *Psychology Today, 22*(5), 18–20.

Engman, R. (1992, January). On a roll: A successful after-school tutoring program at (Patrick Henry School, Alexandria, Virginia). *Principal, 71,* 24–25.

Footlick, J. K. (1990, Winter/Spring). What happened to the family? *Newsweek,* 14–18.

Frymier, J., & Gansneder, B. (1989). The Phi Delta Kappa study of students at-risk. *Phi Delta Kappan, 71,* 142–146.

Giroux, Henry (1983). *Theory of resistance: A pedogogy for the opposition.* South Hadley, MA: Bergin and Garvey.

Henderson, D. (1990, May/June). Expanding the curriculum with after-school classes, Oak Park Valley Union Elementary School District, Tulare, California. *Thrust, 1,* 32–33.

Hollingshead, A. B. (1949). *Elmstown youth.* New York: John Wiley and Sons.

Ingrassia, Michel et al. (1993, August). Endangered family. *Newsweek, 30,* 17–26.

Jacoby, M. D. (1986, November). School improvement and after-school programs: Making the connection. *Middle School Journal, 18,* 3–8.

Kohl, M. J. (1991, January/February). After-school latchkey program. *Teacher of Home Economics, 34,* 104.

Kohn, Melvin. (1969). *Class and conformity: A study of values.* Homewood, IL: Dorsey.

Ledman, S. M. et al. (1991). The every buddy program: An integrated after-school program. *Child Today* (no. 2), 17–20.

Lehman, Irving J., & Mehrens, W. H. (1970). *Educational research reading in focus.* New York: Holt, Rinehart and Winston.

Mercure, M. (1993, September). Project Achievement: An After-school success story. *Principal, 73,* 48–50.

Merton, Robert. (1948). The self-fulfilling prophesy. *Antioch Review, 8,* 193–210.

Milch, N. (1986, September). After-math: A program for after-school help. *NAASP Bulletin, 70,* 107–9.

Morris, D. et al. (1990, November). Helping low readers in grades 2 and 3: An after-school volunteer tutoring program. *Elementary School Journal, 91,* 132–50.

Moyers, S. (1993, February). Turned on to school. *Instructor, 102,* 50–52.

Nemeth, P. (1992, November). The art of learning (Arts partners after-school program in New York City). *American Teacher, 77,* 7.

Nieto, Sonia. (1992). *Affirming diversity: The sociopolitical context of multicultural education.* New York: Longmans.

Pariso, A. (1991, January). School climate and student motivation for academic excellence (After-school program at Killian High School, Miami, Florida). *NAASP Bulletin, 75,* 101–12.

Schine, J. G. (1989, January/February). Adolescents help themselves by helping others: The early adolescent helper program. *Children Today, 18,* 10–15.

Seligmann, J. (1990, Winter/Spring). Variation on a theme. *Newsweek,* 38–40, 44, 46.

Sherraden, W. (1992). School dropouts in perspective. In K. Ryan & J. Cooper (Eds.), *Kaleidoscope; Readings in education* (6th ed.) (pp. 93–103). Boston: Houghton-Mifflin.

Wasserman, Miriam. (1970). *The school fix: New York City, USA.* New York: Outerbridge and Dienstfrey.

Webb, L., Metha, A., & Jordan, K. (1992). *Foundations of American education.* New York: MacMillan.

Wellhousen, K. (1993, Annual issue). Children from non-traditional families: A lesson in acceptance. *69,* 287–88.

Wilson, A. B. (1989, Summer). Theory into practice: An effective program for urban youth (Interface Institute). *Educational Horizon, 67,* 136–44.

Part I

GETTING STARTED

THE ORGANIZERS

An *after-school* educational enrichment program can be started in most any community where there is a need. A single person may observe and sense the need for the service. Some indicators of possible need are communities where children are seen strolling the streets and *hanging out* on street corners—in front of businesses and at local malls in the hours after school; homes where there are two working parents and single-parent families whose income levels may not allow them to provide paid after-school supervision for their children; neighborhood schools where students' standardized test scores are known to be below expectations as well as neighborhoods where significant numbers of youth commit offenses against society—all suggest that youth are in need of help. More often it can be found that the children in the conditions and behavior modes noted are also children who are failing or near failing in school and manifest behavioral problems in their school and home environments.

Many children who have not yet become problems in schools and the home are *at risk* because of the factors in their environment that daily whittle away at their person and their resolve.

The one person who senses the need for after-school services in the community may choose to talk to a variety of community leaders and representatives of agencies that serve children and families. Personnel of local social services agencies may be consulted. These staffs can identify families and individual children with specific needs. Schools and teachers are a primary source for consultation about the students that attend the schools. Teachers know children who are in need of additional academic help, and counselors of the schools know of children with problems that are both academic and social. The local schools must be a major partner in the after-school program. Church leaders and members of churches may know of families in the church community and/or nearby communi-

15

ties who have children that need help. Civic and social organizations often have community advisors who work with the community and have insights on children's needs in specific segments of the community. Public housing personnel in most communities have a range of staffs that work with families in the housing complexes. These individuals have a good grasp of youth needs and they, as well as the residents and resident counselors, are key sources for a range of information that would help the *organizing* person gain more insights on the issue.

Persons working at recreation centers may observe children who appear to like or dislike school, children who seem aimless and are not participating in the recreational activities, and children who attempt to do homework at the center.

Libraries receive children after school, some who come and spend the afternoon until called for or until they decide to leave. Many of these children seek the librarian as a *homework assistant/tutor*. Children in these circumstances should be able to go to an after-school program with staff with time that more nearly meets their needs.

Having interviewed and talked with a variety of community personalities, educators, and parents, and having read a significant number of works on education, child development, and community service, the *organizing person* should have a better grasp of what he or she sees needs to be done and possibly how to go about getting some things done. By now, the *organizing person* may want to approach another person to share the concerns, insights and interest expressed to date. These persons form the *organizing pair*. The pair may explore an area that could be served: a school community, recreation center, library, church, public or private housing complex, the YMCA and YWCA, and other potential agencies and locations to determine if similar programs exist in the community and the feasibility of setting up a new or additional service in the area.

The community under consideration should evidence a student population of about fifty or more potential enrollees. Of the potential enrollees, an average of twenty-five children or so are likely to become participants in the program. Dropout rates for after-school enrollees are about ten to fifty percent.

By the time the pair has identified a potential *community to serve,* it will recognize the need to expand its number. Three to five additional enthusiastic and competent persons may be asked to join the pair. The *organizing persons* are now a group of five to seven persons and may turn their attention to becoming a formally organized *body*. The group may utilize a number of human and materials resources to assist in becoming a *community* organization.

As the organizing body works with its organizational structure, it continues its purpose in studying and preparing for the after-school program. The body will soon find it feasible to appoint an *advisory council* to assist and advise in the finalizing of the key elements of the program's planning.

THE ADVISORY COUNCIL

The Advisory Council should include a broad range of persons who have specific training, skills, and insights required to develop and implement an *after-school* program. These persons should include curriculum specialists, statisticians, fund raisers, public relations personnel, developmental psychologists and parent education specialists, parents, and citizens at large. Many persons have multiple skills and dual areas of specialties. Therefore, a psychologist may also be a parent educator and have a background in child development. A public relations person may also have skills in organizational management. A minister may know curriculum and even be a classroom teacher. The point is to determine the specific skills that members of the council may need in order to effectively deliberate the concerns that the program should address, keeping in mind that some individuals have multiple skills and competencies. However, some skills are so critical that a single individual within a highly specialized area may represent only that specialty. Care must be taken to put together a group of people who can work together. A group of *grandstanders* who are not team builders, despite their skills, and who do not buy into an after-school service concept can sabotage the effort.

The organizing group may suggest that the council set forth bylaws governing terms of office of its members, numbers and titles of officers and their duties, duties of members, frequency of meetings, and scope and role of the council. On the other hand, the organizing group may have in mind how it wishes to see the council work and devise guidelines to be presented to the council.

When the advisory council is in place, the organizing group may disband. It may also continue as a sponsoring body or it may turn the helm over to an existing organization for sponsorship. The rules of the organizing group may be written as to allow a percentage of organizing members to continue on the *advisory council* if they meet the criteria determined by the group. Some organizing members may wish to continue, while some others, feeling that certain objectives have been met, may elect to withdraw. It is critical, however, that those who have laid the foundation not be perceived as expendable. Certainly, the person who conceived of the idea should remain as a key figure, and due recognition should be accorded this person. Care must always be taken to involve the people who are to be served, utilizing them in planning and decision making and avoiding limiting them to roles of manual tasks, and finding ways to incorporate their ideas and assisting them in defining and articulating their ideas. Shaping a community program that is top-heavy with *specialists,* without the people being served feeling that they are equal partners, dooms the project to less than its full potential.

As the council's work moves closer to the program's implementation, more specific goals must be defined. The council should now turn to the larger community, opening up the after-school idea for discussion, seeking the public's perception of its needs, individual's perceptions of their needs, and the established institution's view of community needs.

Community Input

The community-based after-school program must seek the advice and consent of the community it plans to serve, and it must get insights and perspectives from the people who will be affected. This input may be sought and acquired through a variety of means including: interviews, surveys, questionnaires, public meetings, etc. Each approach should be innovative and may utilize varying techniques.

A committee, individual, or agency undertaking the interview process plans may interview selected individuals who represent specific interests and agencies in the community such as school personnel, social services staff, church leaders, civic and social personalities, and business leaders. Additionally, parents, students, and citizens at large should be included in the activities.

Surveys and questionnaires may be designed to elicit a range of responses from residents in the community. Door-to-door distribution of questionnaires, mailings of the questionnaires to customers of local businesses, distribution of questionnaires to organizations and churches, and placement of the forms in public places and in the local newspaper help to broaden the base of persons reached.

The efforts in getting the community involved may include a series of public meetings. The public meetings can be in the form of a forum and may also serve as a means to advise and inform. Public meetings allow citizens to meet face-to-face with one another and create a dialogue that generally stimulates new ideas and suggestions. It also provides a forum for people who may not otherwise get an opportunity to express themselves in a public setting. Because the forum is an open meeting, the moderator should be prepared to conduct the meetings under rules that are either decided upon by the body gathered or should observe predetermined rules that the moderator announces. These plans help to avoid attempts by individuals who may come to the public meeting with their own agendas and *axes to grind* that have nothing to do with the forum's purpose.

Whatever format the *input effort* takes, it must stay focused. The design of appropriate instruments for surveys and questionnaires, the formats for interviews, and the public forum plans must be carefully worked out before being put into action. The planning leadership should seek volunteers or paid consultants to assist in designing, implementing, and analyzing the instruments and the feedback from them. The *input* formats should be able to answer the questions: *What information is being sought?* and *How will the information be used?*

Further consideration in planning for *community input* includes scheduling and times for interviews, problems in reaching people who are employed, and selling people on the value of completing a questionnaire or doing an interview.

Transportation for getting interested indigent people to the forums and the provision of *child care* during forum sessions should be considered.

GOALS FOR THE PROGRAM

From the beginning of the idea of an *after-school* program there was a general view of what could be accomplished. The *organizing person* who first presented the idea may have thought: *There are a lot of children hanging around that drugstore after school. Shouldn't there be some place for them to go—not just hanging around? What of their schoolwork? Wonder do they have assignments?* Finally, the observer may conclude: *Those children need to be some place safe with something to do just after school.* This person may have mulled over the thought for a while and then shared it with someone else as noted in the previous section. The second person may well have asked, *What can be done?* And the pair began to generalize and share ideas borne of their own philosophy and what they saw and felt about society, people and youth.

The general concept of the after-school idea must be translated into a relatively precise and uniform statement. This is a challenge. Refining and defining concepts and shaping them into a framework for action is always hard intellectual work. Conflicting solutions are often proposed, and several options may be presented before one is decided upon. There is need to sort among the many options and remedies and settle on specific ones that are *do-able,* or can be accomplished.

The goals that evolve should reflect the relationship between the concept and the reality of the information gathered. Therefore, research and learnings coming from the public through *community input* is invaluable. Insights and experiences shared by the public help the program confirm and validate its purpose. The goal's working efforts ask: What does the community want to do about children who are left to their own devices in the hours after school? What do the people have to say about how they want the efforts carried out? What are the needs of the community as the residents see them, and does the community propose any solutions? When it is determined what should be done, will it be feasible or can it be done given present and potential resources? If it is felt that the goals are achievable, then how to go about *doing* them?

The goal-setting process may begin with such statements as: *To enhance and enrich the lives of youth in the local community. To strengthen the African-American (Hispanic, other) community through supplementary educational and parental involvement experiences.* The goals must specifically point out what needs to be done: (Example) *To provide after-school tutoring and homework assistance to twenty children who live in the Harshaw community.*

The question must follow as to HOW the twenty children will be served. (Example) *To offer supervised homework and one-on-one tutoring to twenty children in the Harshaw community for fifteen hours a week: Monday–Friday 2:30 p.m.–5:30 p.m. at Bingham Memorial Church.* (Example) *To provide a safe environment and a mature, congenial staff that will assist children in their homework and related cultural and social experiences during the hours of 2:30 p.m.–5:30 p.m. Monday–Friday.* Other goals may be stated: *To increase the number of school successes among youth in the Harshaw community and reduce the number of dropouts among at-risk children. To communicate to parents the significance of their involvement and support of their children's education.* As many people as possible, as noted earlier, should have input in the shaping of the goals for the program. The goals and the objectives that will implement the goals will be the guide that determines the scope and limitations of the program.

COOPERATIVE EFFORTS

The community-based *after-school* program should be cooperative efforts on the parts of two or more agencies, organizations, or other entities in the community. Through cooperative efforts the program may be organized, implemented and maintained for as long as the people who make the efforts are willing for it to continue.

Cooperative efforts may be described in the following ways: sponsorship, supporter, and partnership. The sponsoring body can be an existing community organization or a group that makes the decision to organize for the purpose of sponsoring an *after-school program.* The section of this part that deals with the *organizers* discusses how one and two people can begin a grass roots effort to get a program underway.

The **sponsor** assumes responsibility for the program through seeing that it is maintained and has the financial support and staff that are needed to operate effectively. The sponsor is the overseer and guardian body. A committee within an existing organization may be assigned to carry on the work of the sponsoring unit and serve as the liaison between the organization and the program. Churches, community centers, libraries, fraternal and social organizations, civic and benevolent foundations and groups may become sponsors of the program.

Cooperative efforts may be seen in the role of **supporters. Supporters** defend, speak for, and serve as a kind of *cheering squad* for the program. Public leaders in such domains as religion, education, social services, child and family advocate groups, parent-teacher organizations, boys and girls clubs, Boy and Girl Scouts, Young Men and Young Women's Christian Associations, corporations, business leaders, and elected officials should be advised and informed as to the program's goals and objectives and encouraged to be supporters.

Leadership and planning affairs of the program that are open to the public should provide opportunities for *supporters* to be seen and heard. The supporters, with channels into many foundations and related agencies, can benefit the program's efforts in many ways. Good public relations is a key in garnering support, and supporters and other persons with public relations skills should be on the advisory council as noted earlier.

A **partnership** is a relationship existing between two or more persons contractually associated and working toward specific ends. Partners are distinguished by their participatory activities and efforts. These efforts are visible and can be evaluated and measured. Partnerships may be categorized by (1) *financial partnership,* (2) *service partnership,* (3) *resources partnership,* and (4) *parent partnership.* The financial partnership occurs when an agency, corporation, other entities or person(s) commit and contract to provide funds to the program to defray general or specific costs involved in the operation of the program. Funds are more often presented as outright grants or gifts of money that is placed in the account that is or will be set up for the use of the program. These funds may be made available annually as a result of a proposal that has been written and presented to an agency. The agency commits to making funds available in specific amounts and depositing the funds in the program's account each year.

The partnership can be in the way of service. Individuals or agencies may commit or guarantee services to be given to the program through such means as specialists providing consulting time, bookkeeping, and managing advice, individuals serving as day-to-day instructional leaders, persons providing clerical assistance, individuals or groups that commit to providing transportation on a regular basis or on special occasions, and routine repairs of equipment and upkeep of quarters (cleaning, arranging of facilities, etc.).

Other means of partnership include providing facilities/resources, physical quarters, an appropriate place for housing the program. Groups and individuals may also serve as partners in providing food (snacks) for children enrolled in the program. Nourishing snacks of quality foods should be served to all children who are in the program over two hours each day.

Provision of instructional materials on a regular basis can be a partnership effort. Groups, organizations, or individuals may place money in the account of the program for the purpose of purchasing clerical and educational supplies and materials, and/or it may elect to make regular donations of materials in consultation with the staff. When gifts of materials are offered, consulting with the instructional staff is necessary to ensure that the more appropriate educational materials are selected. As the program perceives and articulates its needs, it should actively seek partners to become *contractually* committed and actively involved.

The parent partnership can be implemented through individual or group efforts in any one or more of the above ways and in more specific ways. The difference in this partnership is that parents have children in the program. *Parent partnerships* will be discussed under the Parent Program.

PUBLICITY FOR THE NEW PROGRAM

When the staff has been selected, the quarters readied, and the program plan is in place, the center is ready to open. Effective publicity must be planned and implemented to *get the word around* and participants involved. Publicity should cover the entire community but must be focused with intensity on the target population.

Publicity items and activities should include flyers, brochures, announcements in local newspapers and on radio and television. Guest appearances on public service television and radio provide opportunities for oral explanations of the program and for a personal touch.

Printed materials should be bright and attractive and distributed to churches, schools, public meeting places, clubs, and organizations. Volunteer artists and printers can help in designing attractive eye-catching releases.

The flyer announces the program in broad terms noting what the program is, for whom it is intended, highlights of activities, the hours of service, the location and telephone number. The brochure is more detailed and, in addition to basic information, should include the goals and objectives of the program, major personalities working with the program, anticipated outcomes of the after-school service, and sponsors.

The program may choose a logo and a color that become symbols of the program. Stationery should be printed and it too may choose to follow through on the color scheme and logo.

Advocates and professionals can further the publicity through *word of mouth*. The advisory council and supporters can *talk-up* the program. The Parent Educator and Program Director may visit schools and churches and encourage parents and children to participate. One effective means to reach parents and children is to request school principals to survey teachers for recommendations of students who would benefit from the *after-school* experience. When the parent educator receives the names of children and their parents, he/she should contact the parents to determine their interest in participating in the program. Persons who assumed leadership in the publicity activities for the community input may be called upon to lead or assist in the publicity for the program's opening.

The program should set a time and place for registration for participants and use the time not only to *sign up children* but also to get acquainted with the parents and the children. This is likely to be the initial interview and should involve both parent and child. The *parent commitment* form is presented and explained at this time. The parent then reads the *participant contract* to the child and explains what will be expected of him or her in the center and what the center offers to the child.

FUND RAISING

When the goals of the program are in place and the program has a clear vision of what it wants to do, how it will do it, and what is required to accomplish the tasks, it must speak to the matter of a budget and finances. The *budget* cites the needs and activities of the program as expressed in fiscal terms.

The budget is a document that attests to the need for or the presence of money. Despite the many volunteers and cooperative sharing efforts, an after-school program must have a sound financial base upon which to operate.

Where to get the money? Money is out there. Locating it and convincing donors to give is the challenge. Fund raising is both an art and a skill. Most people can be trained to develop skills in fund raising. Some people are more adept at such tasks than others. Therefore, the program should have both professional fund raisers and volunteer persons involved in grant-seeking efforts. A fund-raising committee with an innovative chairperson may take the helm in identifying funding sources and getting grants and aid.

Major sources for fund raising include:

Foundations
- Private foundations—a private foundation is a non-governmental, non-profit entity having a principal fund of its own.
- Community foundation—a co-op or pool of donor trust funds in a community foundation that is set aside or earmarked for a specific interest in the community.

PARTNERSHIPS IN

CHILD DEVELOPMENT

Home, School, Church ...

Focusing On:

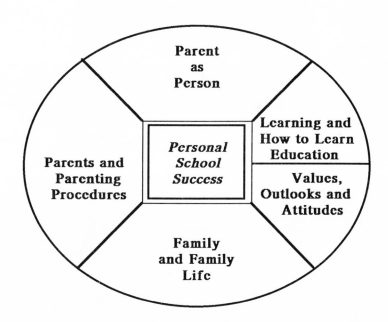

- Corporate foundation—a large company with direct giving practices that also makes contributions to specific causes of its own interest.
- Public foundation—raises money and then awards it to another, thus becoming both a donor and a donee.

- Religious organizations—groups that give money to charities for their own local, national, international work; some grant funds to specific programs in the community specifically for outreach and immediate community concern.
- Benevolent organizations—such grant makers as the United Way that collect money through workplace solicitations and in turn receive grants from private donors.

The process of grant searching begins with a sound proposal. The proposal is similar to a business plan. It must sell the donor on the idea that the program is a good investment. The proposal should emphasize that the program can get results dollar for dollar. The grantor should get the feeling that through its contributions to the program efforts, individuals and the community will be better off; that the funds can help keep children in school and off the streets, or bring families closer together, reduce violence, improve schools, or achieve a number of worthy goals.

A proposal should be written in a positive tone. Although the needs statement must lay out the problem, too much of the negative details can be demoralizing to the point that the donor cannot visualize how his or her money can possibly make a difference.

The proposal should set *measurable goals* and indicate how the results will be measured. The detailed budget in the proposal should state how much money is needed to help achieve the goals, how much money is on hand or can be contributed in *in-kind* contributions, if the proposal is being sent to other funding agencies and what share of the funds is being sought from each. Additionally, the proposal should indicate how the program will be sustained once the grant funds are exhausted. The more effective grant request is one that shows how the requestor plans to *match* the funds sought.

Grants come in various sizes and forms. Planning grants are often awarded to assist a group or organization in getting ready to present a larger grant request or to explore and test some hypothesis before entering into an endeavor full-time. Some grant requests are made for a short-term activity to accomplish a whole or part of a larger effort. During the early stages of after-school organizing efforts, planning grants may be pursued. Since private foundations require that groups making requests give evidence of non-profit status and are tax-exempt under Section 501(c)(3) of the Internal Revenue tax codes, the group can look to other funding sources in the community. The community foundations are an excellent source of funding as well as local businesses and social/civic groups when the groups lack tax-exempt status.

The organizing group may desire to become a permanent body and in so doing it can pursue the *non-profit, tax-exempt* status, since any group supporting a good cause can generally get the tax-exempt status if it is a religious, educational, charitable, scientific, literary, national or international amateur sports organization.

While funds from foundations are eagerly sought, not all funds that are available are in foundations. Local businesses, social groups (fraternity and sorority, bridge and flower clubs, to name a few), civic groups, churches, and philanthropically oriented individuals are good sources to consider for the *funds searching*. Local groups have a stake in the work of human development programs and with planned strategies for appeals, significant funds may be acquired.

A strategy for fund raising by an after-school program is seen in the excerpt from a brochure seeking a *partnership budgeting* approach (see the Section "Partnership Budgeting—Invest in the Future"). Organizations were asked to set a sum of money aside each month for the purpose of supporting the program. The appeal is to **Invest in the Future** and the focus is on *community self-help*. While each organization's sum may be modest, multiplied by several organizations a substantial amount can be assured for operational costs.

Some sponsors of programs hold annual and special events to raise funds. Some of these events become *premiere affairs* in the local community. Holding an event for the purpose of fund raising can accomplish several things: It can gain money, but, if not properly planned and organized, it can also lose money. The event can bring exposure to the program and provide a showcase to recognize volunteers and contributors. The publicity and goodwill potentials for such events are well worth consideration.

Parents with children in the after-school program can assure their *partnership* commitment through fund raising. Parents may sponsor such activities as yard sales, bake sales, sales of crafts and products, car washes in which the youth may participate, *rent-a-husband*, child sitting, and other services for hire.

Volunteers may be called upon to assist in fund-raising efforts. Young professionals, senior citizens, and retired persons are good age groups to seek out to assist in campaigns. Young, successful adults employed in corporations and industries may be *lead-ins* to corporate funding and provide contacts with potential donors. These same persons may be influenced toward personal contributions since many may have children at the age levels of the children served in center programs.

Fund raisers tend to appeal largely to the affluent population. Lower-income persons should be encouraged to participate as well and given decision-making roles in the fund-raising activities.

SAMPLE

Partnership Budgeting

INVEST IN THE FUTURE
An Academic/Cultural Enrichment Program For
African-American Children

This is a program initiative to secure funds from the African-American community to aid at-risk black children and exemplify our historic belief in **SELF-HELP.**

PURPOSE

The purpose of this initiative is to secure funds from twenty-five (25) African-American social/service clubs to sustain After-School Tutorial Enrichment Centers.

While the Center Program looks to public and private sources to secure funds, the African-American community needs to take a stake in its future and give aid and help to efforts to strengthen our black families and the education, training, and development of our black children.

PLAN

The plan is for each organization to budget $100 per month for ten (10) months for five (5) years, making a total contribution of $5,000 to the developmental program for our children. Each organization will be given a certificate (blue) when the first $1,000 is presented or when contributions total $1,000. When the $5,000 have accumulated, the organization will be awarded a plaque.

With options lying before us, we cannot afford to reject these efforts to save our children—invest in the future.

Won't your organization **COMMIT NOW!**

HUMAN RESOURCES

Human resources consider the people who make the program work. The staff and resource personnel are the wheels of the whole endeavor. Without them, the plans and proposals would lie dormant. Before a center opens for service it must have a well-trained, knowledgeable, and caring staff in place. Staff may be of two basic types: *Paid Staff* and *Volunteers.* Both of these kinds of staffs may be called by other names and can be expanded in titles and functions to meet the specific needs of a center and the community.

The sponsoring body and the Advisory Council should study personnel needs based on the plan of the after-school program. The first staff person that may be named is that of the Director of the Program. The Director of the Program may assume the critical task of defining and shaping the staff. The director will be involved in implementing goals and objectives relating to personnel to help ensure that program goals are achieved. Specific jobs and job titles, descriptions of jobs, and qualifications required for each job should be studied with care.

The organizational chart should be designed to show lines of responsibilities and the relationship of each job to the other. (See example: Organizational Chart.)

Paid Staff

Some tutors, the Site Supervisor, and the Program Director are generally paid stipends. The key paid staff member, however, is the Program Director.

The Program Director

As the first paid staff member, the Program Director (PD) assumes the leadership and administrative duties in the center. This person knows and understands children, has good rapport with the community, appreciates the needs of families and parents, and has experience and training in curriculum and teaching. The PD takes the leadership in developing the center's program of activities. He or she identifies staff, prepares training activities, supervises staff work in the center, and oversees learning/teaching plans. In some settings the PD has fund raising as a major responsibility.

Site Supervisor

This is a position that involves the day-to-day supervision and operation of the center program—its staff and participants. The *site supervisor* (SS) has the responsibility of seeing that the center opens at stated hours, that the climate of the center is appropriate, that all materials and furnishings are functional and are in the proper place, that the schedule of the day is followed, that all children are appropriately called for at the end of the day, and that the center is closed and secured until the next use.

Lead Tutor

This position may be a paid or a volunteer post. The paid *lead tutor* (LT) can be expected to be held to an accountability that cannot be required of a volunteer, although volunteers are expected to be as reliable and accountable as a paid person. Working with the SS, the LT trains tutors and volunteers before they begin activities in the center and plans tutors' schedules and assignments based on general and specific needs of students. In cooperation with the site supervisor (SS), the LT monitors learning goals and instructional activities, and sees that appropriate numbers of materials are available for specific and general learning activities. The LT assists in assuring that tutors stay on task in the center and that tutor and tutoree are an appropriate match.

The Parent Educator

The Parent Educator (PE) is the liaison between the center and parents—the child and the school. This person gets to know each child at a more intimate level and works with his parents and teachers. The PE takes the leadership in organizing parents, interviews parents, follows up on parents and child when and if breakdowns occur and discusses needs of child with parents and teachers. The PE makes school visits on a routine basis and works with the local PTA group. Parent seminars are planned by the PE in cooperation with the staff and parents, and parent involvement activities are developed and encouraged by the PE. This person seeks parents as volunteers in the center and serves as parent/child advocate in the community. The PE spends a specific number of hours a week in the center interacting with children and participating in the program's scheduled activities.

Persons who hold the above-named positions represent the minimal size staff. The levels of responsibilities of these positions warrant financial remuneration. Salaries of the center staff are based on *part-time* work, and leadership/administrative pay may be negotiated and based on several current factors, patterns, and practices in the local community. Some centers base the wage scale on the pay for local substitute teachers in the public schools and minimum hourly wage for paid tutors.

Availability of funds and qualifications of the person who holds a position may result in varying salary schedules. Salaries may also fluctuate with the coming and going of grant funds and unique needs that occur. Some programs require the director or coordinator of the program to write proposals and seek grant funds. Thus the person guarantees his or her salary through specific efforts.

Volunteer Staff

Persons who devote time, energy, interests, and talents to after-school and other programs without pay are indispensable. Their services often sustain a program that could not function otherwise, and their examples of caring and sharing inspire others to greater heights of commitment and involvement.

Volunteers may be classified as:

- **Staff** volunteer carries out daily assignments in tutoring, assisting with the serving of snacks, preparing learning materials, typing, etc. (see list of Activities for Volunteers).
- **Resource** volunteer comes to center on occasion and performs certain tasks or makes presentations; person may also assist on field trips, present videos and perform such duties as *reading* to children, storytelling, dramatic skits, foreign language sessions, and puppet making).
- **Consultant** person is one who has specific skills and training and advises and consults with the director and other staff, offers services for such tasks as preparation of budget and tax reports, staff training, etc.

Staff Qualifications

All persons serving the program are *staff.* Volunteer staff (VS) are unpaid. Main staff is paid. Staff, whether paid or volunteer, should possess certain basic human qualities and characteristics. Additionally, other qualifications may be required to ensure compatibility with the roles and responsibilities to be assumed. All persons in service-giving activities must respect and appreciate people. Persons working with youth must have an understanding of growth and development cycles of youth and appreciate their unique needs. A person working in an *after-school* program must have a genuine respect for **education** and perceive the place it has in the growth and development of children. This person should also perceive education as a lifelong learning experience and relate education as a continuum. The *after-school* staff person should have effective communication skills, competence in basic learning skills, ability to learn new facts, interest in and enthusiasm for the center program, and the ability to work as a member of a team.

The staff must believe in the value of the program's work efforts and visualize how it can effect changes in youth and parents' lives. Despite staff training and experience, without commitment to the program goals and efforts, a staff member can become a hindrance rather than a help.

Occasionally, individuals apply for part-time work in programs and their biases are discovered in the interview. It is the perception of some few people that a *community-based* program designed to provide educational experiences for students must be populated by youth who have serious behavioral, academic, or social problems. Thus, the staff, paid or volunteer, must be open-minded about the circumstances of children and avoid stereotypical conclusions.

It is a good practice to utilize volunteers and paid consultants in developing human resources or personnel guidelines, procedures, and records.

Application forms should be designed and available and each person that seeks a job in the center should complete one. Provisions for information on schooling, prior work experience, and character references should be included. It is critical that the personnel process follow up on personal references to assure that only the appropriate persons are selected to be placed among the youth.

Suggested Educational Requirements for Leadership Staff

A person who serves as the director must have a high school diploma and some college training. Graduates of technical/junior college programs in child development are good candidates. Optimally speaking, persons who are former teachers, teacher aides, and teachers themselves who seek part-time employment are excellent candidates.

The SS must hold a high school diploma or an equivalent and evidence basic educational skills competence. This person should evidence abilities to plan and supervise. Teacher assistants are good candidates for this post.

The PE should hold a high school diploma or an equivalent and have completed courses in sociology and community work. This person should show evidence of having attended workshops in *parenting education* and preferably hold a college degree. The PE, like the director, must work with schools and be abreast of curriculum contents and trends. Persons who have good potentials for certain positions such as the PE can be assisted in becoming prepared for the job through support from the program to take courses and attend professional meetings.

Tutors should have completed at least three grades above the student being assisted. High school students are often utilized as tutors. The LT in the center should assure that any tutor is capable of the tasks he or she assumes. Tutors should be monitored and a follow-up procedure should be provided to assure that the process is effective.

While a high school diploma is generally a *basic* qualification for tutoring and high school students tutor under more direct supervision, there are persons who may serve as *volunteers* in the center based on their positive, personal experiences. These persons may have little formal training but demonstrate by their lives and contributions that they are persons worthy to be emulated. Such persons make good **mentors.** These persons include heads of stable families, church leaders, business owners, community volunteers, housewives, fathers and mothers, lay and professional people—skilled and unskilled persons.

STAFF RECRUITMENT AND TRAINING

An effective recruitment process should produce the right number and right kind of new personnel at the right time so that the program's needs are met. Generally this section refers to paid staff (PS).

Before recruitment begins, the program must determine what jobs are to be filled and what the requirements are in terms of employee education, experience, skills, and abilities.

Recruitment plans should be formalized and the process set in place and followed. The PD and/or SS may take the major responsibility in recruitment. Other staff may make referrals and recommendations by submitting names of persons. Sponsors and supporters may also recommend staff.

The program may recruit staff from:

1. Referrals
2. Walk-in applicants
3. Advertising in local newspapers and other media
4. Announcements sent to organizations, churches; posted in public places
5. Civic and social clubs
6. Schools and colleges
7. Employment agencies
8. Senior citizens groups
9. Retired persons and organizations (local AARP units)

Some nationally recognized organizations such as the Junior League and Jaycees provide volunteer service as part of the organization's community services. Volunteer recruitment can be assisted by local volunteer action agencies. These agencies generally have developed plans for recruitment, training and placement and can be an excellent resource.

All staff should have job descriptions and complete training sessions before being assigned to specific jobs. A training manual should be developed and used in training so that uniform experiences and information will be shared and learned by trainees.

Sample Job Description

Each person that performs a designated task and is assigned specific duties and responsibilities in the program should have a job description. A *job description* indicates the tasks and duties to be performed on the job, the materials and equipment used, interaction with others, and the kind of supervision required.

After School Tutorial/Enrichment Program
Job Description

TITLE: Site Supervisor
SUPERVISOR: Program Director

1. General Description:
   The overall objective of the Tutorial/Enrichment Program is to provide a quality environment in which each child does his home-

Sample Chart of Organization

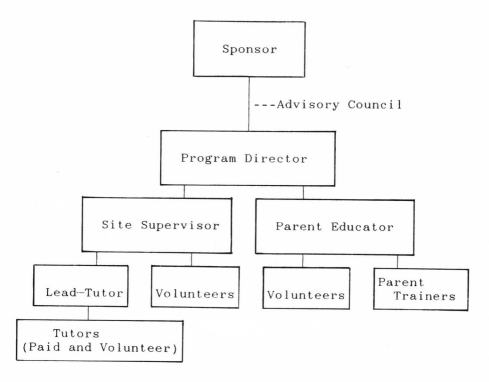

work, learns to appreciate his heritage, develops basic learning skills, and shares with parents in learning. The Site Supervisor's role is to aid in attaining the overall objectives.

2. Responsibilities
   a. Get to know each child in the program and where said child is functioning in his studies
   b. Supervise all homework assignments
   c. Ensure the supervision of enrichment folders
   d. Ensure that children have extra practice work in basic skills
   e. Provide, when possible, additional weekly programs of enrichment activities
   f. Ensure a physical environment that is safe and clean
   g. See that staff arrive at job site on time
   h. Hold monthly staff meetings
   i. Prepare all required reports at the end of each month
   j. Cooperate with parents and parent educator

    k. Ensure data folders for each child. Folder must contain:
1. application form
2. emergency information
3. parent commitment form
4. participant commitment form
5. copy of child's report card
6. student evaluation

    l. Maintain good working relationships with landlord of the facility, i.e., church, housing authority, community center, other

   m. Maintain ongoing inventory of supplies and requisition in advance of need

    n. Maintain confidentiality of records

    o. Ensure that a parent meeting is held at least every other month

    p. Develop an ongoing communication system with each parent

    q. Inspect building and grounds for cleanliness, needed repairs, and general upkeep; open and close center daily

    r. Report all problems to appropriate sources

    s. Ensure that center is attractive to the eye

    t. Identify and recommend staff

3. Qualifications
    a. High school diploma with preference for a degree in elementary education or a subject field
    b. Some college and an understanding of elementary subjects
    c. Some previous experience as a tutor, teacher, or teacher assistant, and an understanding of elementary subjects and basic educational skills
    d. Classroom management skills
    e. Demonstrated ability to organize and implement procedures essential to the operation of a tutorial center
    f. Pleasing personality

4. Hours of service

    The Site Supervisor's schedule is 2:00 p.m.–6:00 p.m. Monday–Friday. The center's program operates concurrently with the public school calendar

PHYSICAL RESOURCES

The *after-school* program must have a physical location. Schools, churches, recreation centers, YMCA's or YWCA's, and clubhouses of organizations are among places the center can be housed.

In choosing a place, the geographic location should be viewed as a critical factor. A center should be located near the homes of children who will attend. Selecting a site on a school bus route and near public transportation lines reduces problems students and parents may have with transportation.

The center site may be a room or suite of rooms that can accommodate a number of children for two to three hours a day. If at all possible, a minimum number of square feet should be provided for each child. The quarters should be on the ground floor and have at least two exits and windows that can be opened. A kitchen or *nook* with running water, refrigerator, and cooking stove should be available for the preparation of snacks. The *place* should be a stable site where materials and equipment can remain intact from September to May. The temperature should be adjustable for varying weather conditions. First-aid and fire-extinguishing supplies and equipment should be available.

The quarters should be bright and well lighted. Floors should be of vinyl or carpet. Chairs and tables should be of an appropriate height to accommodate the age and size of children. Restroom facilities should have running water for hand washing and disposable towels. It should be separate for boys and girls.

Shelves for books and other learning materials should be available. Audiovisual equipment such as overhead projectors, slide projectors, tape players, film projectors and video players should be on hand. Computers and typewriters are desirable. Bulletin boards and chalkboards are needed. Storage cabinets provide a place to *put away* or secure small, perishable items and portable files.

Furnishings and equipment can be purchased or contributed. Furnishings/equipment should be clean, sturdy and appropriate but need not be new. School discards of desks, tables and chairs may be received. Volunteers may repair and refinish gifts of furniture and restore them to excellent states.

MATERIALS RESOURCES

The after-school center should be a *safe place* to be during the hours immediately after school. Providing a safe place to be is only one goal. The center should not be a *child sitting* service but an organized, structured program where teaching and learning take place.

An effective after-school program must have a functional collection of learning resources. These resources should include print and non-print media and appropriate educational equipment.

Dictionaries. Dictionaries are basic learning materials that must be included in the collection. A center that lacks dictionaries is likely not achieving measurable changes in students' learning behaviors. There should be at least two dictionaries for each group table or grade group. It is desirable to have even more. Dictionaries should be appropriate for the age and grade level of students.

Encyclopedias. At least one encyclopedia set should be available. The encyclopedia(s) should be designed for school-age children and where possible be of recent date. In the absence of a current set, an earlier edition may be used.

Thesaurus and rhyming words volumes should be available in the center.

Trade books should be maintained in the collection with a variety of subjects, interests, and grade reading levels represented. Copies of textbooks should also be available.

Magazines selected should include current youth publications and issues on travel, popular magazines, hobbies and crafts. Magazines of such organizations as the Girl and Boy Scouts should also be available.

Television(s) should be available with capability for video playing and recording.

Radio(s), a tape player, and film and slide projectors are needed.

Computers are a MUST in today's learning environment. Computers and the use of them are becoming a common experience in everyday life.

Workbooks and other activity, study, drill, and recreational materials should be available in ample numbers to ensure that no student is left at *loose ends* without something constructive to do.

Games, learning and recreational, can provide students with a variety of experiences. Interactive videos hold children's attention and have the potential for increasing learning. Recreational games can teach math and science concepts as well as language and social studies. Still other games aid in teaching values and social skills. Games are also available that help children develop higher self-esteem and learn more about their cultural heritage.

Artifacts, models, and objects are also learning resources. Children and their parents as well as neighbors and friends have varied materials found in their homes and communities that can be added to the collection or displayed at special times.

The *resources (learning) packages* should be stocked with activity materials that reinforce subject matter and related learnings. The packages may hold the materials or have a bibliography inserted to indicate where other materials are located.

The after-school center should maintain a learning resources center/station or library station where students may withdraw materials for use in the center or checked out for home use. A parent materials collection may be part of the center library, and both parent and child may practice the art of *checking out* learning materials.

The after-school program operating on a limited budget may ponder how to secure the variety of learning materials and resources desired and needed to facilitate educational enrichment. A major consideration that the program will make is that of identifying sources for and securing gifts.

Many public and private schools, as they update their collection, have discards that are in good condition. As newer editions of workbooks, text and trade books are issued, local schools may make contributions to the after-school program upon request. Some publishers share materials that are not in the line of sales, and individuals may make gifts of money or materials.

Some corporations and local companies tend to maintain state-of-the-art technology and replace computers and other hardware at intervals and make gifts of the outdated equipment. Many of the models and pieces of equipment are functional, although not the latest. Some national organizations have as a local service assisting groups in locating and securing sources of pre-owned equipment.

For a list of publishers and suppliers of other materials, see Part IV, "Resources Directory," of this book.

REFERENCES

Blumfeld, S. (1986). *How to tutor* (2nd ed.). New Rochelle, NY: Arlington House.

Clark, S. (1985). *Discover total resources.* Pittsburgh: Community Affairs, Mellon Bank.

Churden, H., & Sherman, W. (1980). *Personnel management: The utilization of human resources* (6th ed.). Cincinnati, OH.

Cox, F. et al. (Ed.). (1987). *Strategies of community organization. A book of readings* (4th ed.). Itasca, IL: Peacock.

Cuban, L. (1989). The at-risk label and the problem of school reform. *Phi Delta Kappan, 70,* 780–84.

Ehly, S., & Larsen, S. (1980). *Peer tutoring for individualized instruction.* Boston: Allyn and Bacon.

Flanagan, J. (1982). *The grassroots fund raising book. How to raise money in your community.* Chicago: Contemporary Books.

—— (1981). *The successful volunteer organization.* Chicago: Contemporary Books.

Gentry, C. S., Jr. (1982). *How to develop a volunteer program for single adults.* Jacksonville, FL: Volunteer Jacksonville, Inc.

George, C. S., Jr. (1985). *Supervision in action. The art of managing others* (4th ed.). Reston, VA: Reston.

Haile, S. (Ed.) (1991). *National directory of corporate giving: A guide to corporate giving programs and corporate foundations* (2nd ed.). Foundation Center.

Hall, M. (1988). *Getting funded: A complete guide to proposal writing* (3rd ed.). Portland, OR: (State) University.

Jackson, J. H., & Keavney, T. (1980). *Successful supervision.* Englewood Cliffs, NJ: Prentice-Hall.

Kramer, R. M., & Specht, H. (1983). *Reading in community organization practice* (3rd ed.). Englewood Cliffs, NJ: Prentice-Hall.

Krase, J. I. (1982). *Self help and community in the city.* Washington, DC: University Press of America.

Levey, J. F. (1983). *If you want air time. A publicity handbook.* Washington, DC: National Association of Broadcasters.

Mehr, J. (1988). *Human services. Concept and intervention strategies* (4th ed.). Boston: Allyn and Bacon.

Mizio, E., & Delaney, A. J. (Eds.). (1981). *Training for service delivery to minority clients.* New York: Family Service Association of America.

National Education Association. Commission on the Reorganization of Secondary Education. (1918). *Cardinal principles of secondary education.* The Association.

Nieto, S. (1992). *Affirming diversity. The sociopolitical context of multicultural education.* New York: Longmans.

Phillips, D. C., & Soltis, J. F. (1985). *Perspectives on learning.* New York: Teachers College, Columbia University.

Portelli, J. P. (1992). On defining curriculum. *Journal of Curriculum and Supervision, 2,* 357–67.

Public Management Institute (1980). *The quick proposal workbook.* San Francisco: The Institute.

—— (1979). *Successful public relations techniques.* San Francisco: The Institute.

Robert's Rules of Order (Newly Rev.) (1981), Sarah Corbin (Ed.). Glenview, IL: Scott, Foresman.

Ross, M. (1958). *Case histories in community organization.* NY: Harper.

Samuda, R. (Ed.), & Shies, K. (1986). *Multicultural education programs and methods.* Toronto: Intellectual Social Sciences Publications.

Schaefer, E. S. (1969). A home tutoring program. *Children, 16*(2), 59–61.

Stark, T. (1990). *Innovative grassroots financing: A small town guide to raising funds and cutting costs.* Washington, DC: National Association of Towns and Townships.

Swanson, M. (1991). *At-risk students in elementary education. Effective schools for disadvantaged learners.* Springfield, IL: Charles C Thomas, Publisher.

Taylor, D., & Strickland, D. (1986). *Family storybook reading.* Portsmouth, NH: Heinemann.

Thayer, L. (1981). *Fifty strategies for experiential learning. Book two.* San Diego, CA: University Associates, Inc.

Topping, K. (1989). Peer tutoring and paired reading: Combining two powerful techniques. *The Reading Teacher, 42,* 488–494.

Torre, R., & Bendixes, M. (1986). *Direct mail fund raising. Letters that work.* New York: Plenum Press.

Tyler, R. W. (1949). *Basic principles of curriculum and instruction.* Chicago: University of Chicago Press.

Vail, E. (1967). *Tools of teaching: Techniques for stubborn cases of reading, spelling and behavior.* Springfield, IL: Charles C Thomas, Publisher.

Walberg, H. et al. (1985, April). Homework's power effects on learning. *Educational Leadership,* 76–79.

Weiner, M. (1990). *Human services management, analysis and application* (2nd ed.). Belmont, CA: Wadsworth Publishing.

Part II

THE AFTER-SCHOOL PROGRAM PLAN

The *after-school* program must have a blueprint, or a guide, that shows *what it does* from day to day. One way of describing *what it does* or what goes on in the program is to refer to the activities as the *program plan.* The *program plan* is a framework for achieving the goals, step by step, through the integration of each of the program's components. The *program plan* generally focuses on tutoring and guidance of children in: academic areas where strength is needed, assisting students with homework assignments, aiding in reinforcing basic learning skills, employing techniques in how to learn, demonstrating how to use resources, and guiding students in special efforts and projects.

Three major forces should influence the center's *program plan:* (a) local and state guidelines or standards for *passing a grade* in public schools; (b) basic learnings that are expected and are common knowledge for individuals at certain stages in life; and (c) social/cultural/psychological needs and learnings unique to social groups and/or individuals being served.

The program needs a *program planning committee* to help determine the *program* goals and activities. This committee should be headed by a person with knowledge and experience in the area of the curriculum, supplemented by at-large volunteers and paid or volunteer specialists. The membership of the committee should represent a cross-section of the community. The members of the committee should study basic philosophical works in education and reports of foundations and commissions that have undertaken studies as national educational goals-setting projects. The committee members should read classic and current works on the role of schools in society, the meaning of *public education —* what it is and what it can and cannot do; writings on how schools operate and critiques of studies on inequities in public school education including reports on how diverse youth are performing in schools and society.

The committee also needs to collect and study curriculum guides and sample lesson plans. Its work should include a study of the curriculum of the local school district and it should analyze annual and special reports on students' progress or lack of it. Special attention should be given to the performances of *needs groups.*

The committee should study the community and the families and children that live in the community—their strengths and weaknesses. This body should know who the children and parents are, where they come from, and what the families in the community are confronting. Consideration should be given as to how the program can help youth make the most of their lives.

The committee should communicate with and seek and receive recommendations and advice from local school leaders about ways to interface efforts and what to consider in the *program plan.*

Members of the committee as well as the future staff should attend professional conferences, develop and hold seminars and training sessions for staff, and provide opportunities for staff to better understand and appreciate diversity of groups and persons even of the same racial/ethnic groups. The staff must appreciate cultural differences among youth and be interested in the cultural history of each child served. Although many youth may look alike in dress, hairstyles, speech, and clothing, many differences exist between them in their ways of learning, motivations to learn, and attitudes toward education in general.

Effective learning occurs in a multitude of settings. The *after-school* and *out-of-school* (Maeroff, 1989) programs can be quite meaningful and challenge the school experience, because the instruction is more informal than in school and the experiences tend to be more relaxed.

EXPLORING THE SUBJECT MATTER CONTENTS

The *after-school* program should not seek to be a substitute for the schools. It should seek to supplement and enhance the schooling experience. In order to be an effective partner with the schools in accomplishing effective educational experiences for youth, the *after-school* staff should come away from its studies and critiques of educational information sources with a deeper appreciation and understanding of the whole educative process.

As the *program planning* committee sets about its work, it needs to understand the basic component in any educational endeavor: the *curriculum.* Education specialists on the committee will aid the group by clarifying many points and terms generally cited in learning settings. Curriculum as a term has over a hundred definitions. Simply put, *curriculum* may be defined as all of the educational experiences of students that take place in a school. Curriculum is the framework for getting the work of the school done—for accomplishing the goals set by a school district or local school. *School* may be a term extended to include most settings for learning and the transmission of information, knowledge, or specific skills.

Many models of curriculum exist. In response to criticisms that the schools have not been meeting the educational needs of students, the *back-to-basics* curriculum has received great attention during the last few years. The *back-to-basics* curriculum is basically an *essentialistic* curriculum in that it places emphasis on the *essentials:* reading, writing, and computation. Examination of the literature critical of the current education scene reveals such facts as: (1) American students have shorter school days than youth of other nations; (2) the most effective use of time is not made in school; and (3) schools do not do enough to help students develop in the basic study and learning skills required to master ongoing and successful learning. Additionally, critics believe that decline in student achievement and student failure may be related to the trend in automatic promotion of many marginal students, a broad range of popular but often less meaningful electives taken in school, and textbooks that are more pictorial and less informative and designed to entertain more than educate. Children who are *at risk* in their social environments tend to be impacted more by failures and weaknesses in the educative process.

The public schools are generally organized around kindergarten, elementary, middle and high school. Studies of various guides of state and local school organization and curriculum reveal the following:

Kindergarten is designed to introduce children of age five to new and expanded social relationships and cooperative work/play. The typical kindergarten includes activities involving physical fitness, social relations, science, performing arts, current events, development of a positive self-concept, pre-reading and pre-math activities.

Play is the medium through which most of the kindergarten learnings take place.

The *elementary* school has been historically organized into grades with a grades 1–8 pattern. Today most elementary schools have a K–6 as the most typical pattern. Still another common pattern is K–3 (early childhood–primary grades); 4–6 (upper elementary).

The core of the elementary school curriculum includes reading, writing (including spelling and grammar), mathematics, physical and social sciences. The curriculum also includes some attention to the arts, music, and physical education.

The transition to *junior high* or *middle school* is a major one in the life of a child. It calls for major adjustments and is sometimes traumatic as well. Academic as well as social challenges confront youth during this period. Basic or core courses are presented in the curriculum including physical sciences, health, English, mathematics (algebra and geometry), physical education and sometimes a foreign language. Electives may include home economics, graphics, and crafts. The curriculum at this stage usually includes more specialized resources for subjects in such areas as science, homemaking, and industrial arts.

Between fifth and ninth grades, youngsters generally enter the period of life known as adolescence. During this period youth are likely to have their first encounters and experiments with substances, relationships, and environments that can impact their lives forever. These youth more typically have turbulent emotional swings, rapid physical growth and hormone changes, and are in search of their roles as males and females. These difficulties are compounded by upheavals in society as regards values and expectations of youth. Youth whose home environments are unstable and who lack parent/family support are likely to *drop out* of school before the end of the middle school period.

The *high school* is an enlarged version of middle school. Originally, high school in America reflected a strong academic program. Today's high schools are designed to offer not only programs of academic preparation for college and specialized programs leading to terminal trades proficiency, but a good general education.

Subjects/courses may include:

> English
> United States History
> World History
> Social Problems
> Mathematics
> Science
> Physical Education
> Health
> American Studies
> Biology
> World Culture
> Humanities

Chemistry
Business Education
Reading
Foreign Language
Physical Education
Family Living
Speech and Journalism

Studies of teachers' master schedules of course offerings, lists of topics selected for discussion, skills desired to be developed, textbooks used, and tests and quizzes administered reveal that most schools place dominant emphasis on teaching basic language skills and mastery of mechanics—capitalization, punctuation, paragraphs, and syllabication. Self-expression and creative thought are encouraged. Lists indicate that various genres are encouraged and writing of personal diaries and journals is emphasized.

Reading instruction often borders on remediation involving mechanics of word recognition, phonics, and vocabulary building.

Mathematics curriculum in lower grades tends to focus almost entirely on basic skills. Social studies tend to sample such basics as map skills, facility in oral expression, understanding of the similarities among cultures; study of colonial America, with themes of history, geography and civics.

Science receives its due share in the *curriculum*. Teachers in the first three grades frequently place the child's personal orientation to the natural world above the child's mere possession of information about science. Other teachers tend to teach topics and methods of science to young children.

The *social/cultural* segment of the *program plan* should be designed with the specific needs of the students enrolled in mind. This segment can be defined as being *beyond school subjects*. This unit or segment of instruction should be threaded into the whole of the after-school program and developed to a level that it becomes an integrated and highly effective tool in helping children develop positive attitudes and high senses of self-esteem. This unit, cultural enrichment, serves to help diminish the sense of *valuelessness* many students experience, as discussed earlier in this work, and helps children find their real worth. Children at risk in society as a result of socioeconomic factors have greater need for the *beyond the school subjects*.

Teachers' lesson plans, curriculum guides, textbooks and other cur-

tive offices of local school districts, and centers in communities where there are colleges and teacher education programs. Teacher materials centers and/or a college library will have curriculum guides and related resources. District offices of state departments of education and some public libraries may also have these materials.

SETTING UP THE CONTENTS

Having studied the various guides and aids, having explored the community, dialogued with teachers and parents, and defined the goals of the program, the program may begin to implement the *instructional contents.* The contents may focus on four or five areas depending on the grade levels of students: language arts, mathematics, science, social studies, and cultural enrichment. The activities/lessons/tutoring may be for reinforcement, remediation, and new experience. The staff should meet in regular sessions to determine how the instruction or tutoring will be accomplished and how it will assess the effectiveness of the experiences at various stages.

One approach is to look at the levels of accomplishment sought:
Is the lesson/tutoring for?:

| | | *New* |
| *Reinforcement* | *Remediation* | *Experience* |

(Complete for each subject/focus area)
A. Language arts
B. Mathematics
C. Science
D. Social science
E. Cultural enrichment

UTILIZING STANDARD CURRICULUM GUIDES OR GRADE PASSING STANDARD GUIDELINES

Study the guide or guidelines for the local schools. Determine the appropriateness of use in the center's work. Determine what the program wishes to utilize.

A. Divide the guideline materials by grade and/or subject. Select resources to complement each grade, subject and activity.
B. Develop packages (folders or boxes) and organize them around the guideline with supplementary materials, including:

Work sheets
Games
Video presentations
Tapes and recordings
Maps
References
Objects, facsimiles, models
Others

C. Introduce tutors to the concept of the *packages.* Train them in their use and ensure that systematic use is made of the resources
D. Hold training sessions on how to use materials
E. Monitor tutor effectiveness in *package* use
F. Develop plans for assessing the effective use of the guidelines:
   Time frames for assessment:

   1. daily
   2. weekly
   3. monthly
   4. annually

The following are excerpts from the Greensboro (now Guilford County Schools, North Carolina) Grade Passing Standards.

GPS
LANGUAGE ARTS PROMOTION STANDARDS
Grade 1

Mastery for Language Arts Standards is defined as an average of 70% or higher on all assignments and tests relating to the standard. The standards do not list all of the things that children are taught or all of the things to which they are exposed. Rather, the grade level standards show some of the things most students are able to do after they have successfully completed that grade. Some children will learn how to do these things earlier or later than others.

	Standards	Curr. Guide	Cat-E Level 11
1.	Writes in manuscript first and last name using correct letter for on lined paper.	p. 1–10	No

2. Writes upper- and lowercase letters on lined paper from memory using random dictation.   p. 1–11   No

3. Copies words and sentences using correct letter form on lined paper.   p. 1–11   No

4. Identifies asking and telling sentences orally and recognizes them in written form.   p. 1–1*   Yes

5. Listens and responds in sequence to as many as three directions when given in a group.   p. 1–5e   Yes

6. Uses complete sentences orally and can write a complete sentence.   p. 1–8*   Yes

7. Spells the basic word list in all lessons in Grade 1 spelling book.   No

GPS
LANGUAGE ARTS PROMOTION STANDARDS
Grade 5

Mastery for Language Arts standards is defined as an average of 70% or higher on all assignments and tests relating to the standard. The standards do not list all of the things children are taught or all of the things to which they are exposed. Rather, the grade level standards show some of the things most students are able to do after they have successfully completed that grade. Some children will learn how to do these things earlier or later than others.

Standards	*Curr. Guide*	*Cat-E Level 15*
1. Write sentences together to form a simple paragraph.	p. 4–11, 12*	Yes
2. Spells the basic word list in all lessons in the fifth grade spelling book.		Yes
3. Recognizes and uses adverbs in writing.	p. 5–9, 13*	Yes

*The reference for this skill is *Sequential Steps in Language/Composition,* which is the white supplement to the blue *Communication Arts Resource Guide.*

4. Alphabetizes a list of words beyond the   p. 5–36   Yes
   third letter.
5. Correctly uses periods, commas, and   p. 5–1,2*   Yes
   quotation marks.

GPS
READING PROMOTION STANDARDS
FIFTH GRADE

Mastery for promotion standards is defined as an average of 70% or higher on all assignments and tests relating to the standards. The promotion standards are based on materials and curriculum designated for fifth grade. These standards do not list all of the things children are taught or all of the things to which they are exposed. Rather, the standards show some of the things most students are able to do after they have successfully completed that grade. Some children will learn how to do these things earlier or later than others.

I. Decoding
   The learner will analyze words and understand their meanings using:

   A. Prefixes (fore-, mid-, sub-, super-, trans-, circum-)
   B. Suffixes (-ance, -ant, -en, -an, -hood, -ian, -ship, -ward)
   C. Roots

II. Vocabulary
   The learner will increase vocabulary as an aid to comprehension using:

   A. Contextual clues
   B. Words with multiple meanings
   C. Synonyms
   D. Antonyms
   E. Homonyms
   F. Life Skills word list

III. Comprehension
   The learner will increase comprehension of the written language using the following skills:

---

*The reference for this skill is *Sequential Steps in Language/Composition,* which is the white supplement to the blue *Communication Arts Resource Guide.*

   A. Identifying main idea
   B. Identifying supporting details
   C. Drawing conclusions
   D. Sequencing
   E. Predicting outcomes
   F. Identifying cause and effect
   G. Recognizing character traits
   H. Identifying fact and opinion
   I. Identifying implied meanings

GPS
MATHEMATICS PROMOTION STANDARDS
Kindergarten

Mastery is defined as an average of 70% or higher on the locally developed test assessing that skill or an average of 70% or higher on all assignments and tests relating to that skill. The standards do not list all of the things children are taught or all of the things to which they are exposed. Rather, the grade level standards show some of the things most students are able to do after they have successfully completed that grade. Some children will learn how to do these things earlier or later than others.

Standards	*Curriculum Guide	Merrill Page #	TRB Page #	CAT-E Level 15
1. Matches a number with a corresponding set of physical objects, 1–10.	N-4	15–26 47–58	69–186 129–146	Yes
2. Makes a one-to-one correspondence between two sets, 1–10.	S-1	1–4	45–50	Yes
3. Identifies a circle, square and triangle by name.	G-2	39–42	111–119	Yes
4. Compares sizes: large-small, tall-short, long-short.	G-4	69–70	168–176	Yes

*Note: For each skill, the letter refers to the strand in the curriculum guide for this grade level and the number refers to the skill within the strand. For example, N-4 refers to Numbers, skill 4.

5. Arranges three objects in rank according to size.	S-7	70–72	169, 172, 176, 182	Yes
6. Writes a number when given orally, 1–10.	N-3	Oral		Yes
7. Names, counts, and writes the numbers 1–10 in sequence.	N-2	90, 105	202	Yes
8. Names a penny, nickel and dime.	M-1	117–121	254–262	Yes
9. Gives an example of a day and month.	M-7	113–114		No
10. Sorts geometric objects by color, shape and size.	G-1	31–43 62	99–119	No
11. Identifies positions: top-bottom, over-under, first-last.	G-4	69–78	171–182	No

GPS
MATHEMATICS PROMOTION STANDARDS
Grade 5

Mastery is defined as an average of 70% or higher on the locally developed test assessing that skill or an average of 70% or higher on all assignments and tests relating to that skill. The standards do not list all of the things children are taught or all of the things to which they are exposed. Rather, the grade level standards show some of the things most students are able to do after they have successfully completed that grade. Some children will learn how to do these things earlier or later than others.

Standards	*Curriculum Guide	Merrill Page #	TRB Page #	CAT-E Level 15
1. Names and writes numbers to 1,000,000,000.	N-1	4–7, 18–19 28, 30	64–69 83–85	No
2. States the place value of	N-2	3,6,18–19,	61, 62, 67	Yes

---

*Note: For each skill, the letter refers to the strand in the curriculum guide for this grade level and the number refers to the skill within the strand. For example, N-1 refers to Numbers, skill 1.

		28, 30	83, 85	
each digit in any nine-digit number.				
3. Multiplies a three-digit number by a two-digit number.	O-1	86–87 91	193–195	Yes
4. Solves two-step word problems.	O-7	156–157	300–302	Yes
5. Divides a three-digit number by a one-digit number with remainder.	O-3	114–119	236–244	Yes
6. Determines the average of several numbers.	O-4	122–123	248–250	No
7. Identifies equivalent fractions for a given picture.		194–195	367–369	Yes
8. Determines if an answer is reasonable.		328		Yes
9. Adds and subtracts fractions with like and unlike denominators.	O-6	218–221 228–239	406–411 419–430	Yes
10. Identifies rays and angles.	G-2	166–167	320–322	No
11. Identifies parallel, perpendicular, and intersecting lines.	G-4	170–171	326–327	Yes
12. Names, writes, and orders decimals through tenths.	N-5	291 296–297	523–525 523–534	No

PATTERNS OF INSTRUCTION

Tutoring activities constitute the major portion of time spent with students in the *after-school* center. Not all children in the center program, however, will require tutoring. Some children will need and seek enrichment activities/studies. The program plan should be broad and flexible in that it satisfies the needs of all children enrolled in the program.

In order to meet educational needs of all students enrolled, the *program plan* should consider a variety of instructional approaches in tutoring activities as well as enrichment instruction. The varied approaches may include demonstrations and experiments, gaming and simulation, resource centers, guided discovery, and programmed learning. These patterns and others may be undertaken at the Center/Table in the Age/Grade focuses (see "After-School Program Plan").

Many teachers and educators advocate *direct* or *active* instruction especially in the early grades (Ellis, Cogan, & Howey, 1986). Tutoring is the process of providing *active* and *direct* guidance and instruction to individual students. *Direct* and *active* instruction may be characterized by the following:

- Lessons are structured through review and reteaching.
- Lessons proceed in small steps but at a brisk pace.
- Leader/tutor provides many examples.
- Leader/tutor asks a large number of questions and provides opportunities for practice.
- There is continuous feedback and correction.
- Assignments or activities tend to be short and focused.

Many of the characteristics of *direct* and *active* instruction are also characteristic of recommended *tutoring* methods and approaches. At least the following may be considered as rationales for *direct* and *active* instructional procedures in the *after-school* program:

- Students who come to the center do so for specific purposes.
- Direct attention to specific needs make for the best use of the short time the student is in center.
- Students who need and have not received adequate individualed attention in school can find it in the after-school program.
- Students who are at-risk often have difficulty in concentrating and are prone to distraction. Direct instruction aids the child in developing the ability to focus more effectively.

The *after-school program* has among its goals to aid students in basic skills reinforcement and educational enrichment. Direct and active instruction utilized in appropriate settings and situations with considerations for age and grade levels can be the dominant instructional pattern in reinforcing basic skills in the *after-school* experience.

Reading Skills

Reading Aloud

Reading aloud on a regular basis improves a student's reading, writing, speaking, listening, and imagining skills. Reading aloud with a child is important as well in the child's personal development for it helps to inspire, guide, and educate.

To encourage reading, it is important that the child is interested in the reading material. If the child wants to read, allow the child to help choose the reading material.

Activities

Reading aloud experiences may include:

- Reading a story or play for entertainment
- Reading statements from textbooks on a particular subject
- Reading group announcements aloud
- Reading to classmates
- Reading limericks and nonsense words
- Reading aloud with the use of a tape recorder in order to listen to mistakes made by the reader
- Reading stories and poems aloud and in unison to develop self-confidence and poise.

Reading activities should also be undertaken to help students in:

- Reading to understand charts, maps and graphs
- Reading to differentiate between fact and fiction
- Reading to follow directions
- Reading to get the main idea
- Reading to grasp the sequence of events

Vocabulary Development

Language is one of the major means by which people learn. Vocabulary is one of the chief measuring sticks of intelligence tests. Vocabulary can affect the results of an IQ test (Vail, 1967). Children with limited or impoverished vocabularies are more often less successful in the school experience.

Vocabulary development can be facilitated through the use of a variety of resources, activities and means. Dictionary use is a good place to start in vocabulary building, and the Dolch Word List can be used to create a Word Bank.

The dictionary can be used to identify words, trace word origins, and for punctuation and spelling. Word games can be created out of dictionary use; find matching words (spelling and sound); *n* words or words ending with a particular consonant. Cultural and ethnic heritage can be encouraged through dictionary games. By studying the origins of such words as *okay* (believed to be African in origin), students can be led to new insights into cultures as well as dictionary use. In *after-school* centers, the dictionary should be *presented* each day and be *ever present* during homework and tutoring activities.

Other Vocabulary Building Activities:
- Locate words in newspapers and define.
- Make a vocabulary chart and display new words.
- Work a crossword puzzle.
- Play Scrabble at least once a week.
- Write a play using prefixes and suffixes as characters: let characters interact with *root* word.
- Make up words.
- See how many words can be formed from a single word.
- Find a word for each letter in the alphabet.
- Make flash cards with Word Bank words.
- Use four or more Word Bank words and see how many different sentences can be made with the words.
- Give categories and find a word from the Word Bank that fits into each category.
- Read a menu from a local restaurant.
- Study a menu from a (French, Spanish, Mexican, etc.) restaurant.
- Read *Life Skills* word list (combustible, inflammatory, toxic, etc.).

Writing Skills

Writing is a route to reading effectiveness, a means to develop self-expression, create a tool for understanding, and facilitate learning and discovery. In addition to learning to think well on paper, children learn standard spelling by using words in their own writing. Initially, however, students should be encouraged to get their thoughts on paper.

Activities

- Write a poem or story.
- Keep a journal.
- Make up book stories, poems, and draw pictures.
- Take a comic strip, remove the captions, and write captions.
- Write a paragraph or story to accompany a picture.
- Start a pen pal project.
- Write the first and last sentences of a story or paragraph and have the student fill in the middle.
- Write a story about a picture.
- Write about *places I'd like to go and why.*
- Write about *places I've been.*

Mathematics Skills

Understanding and mastering basic mathematical concepts is the foundation for mastering computation. To help students understand the basic concepts, it is helpful to use concrete objects.

Activities

Use concrete objects like:

- Pennies
- Marbles
- Measuring cups
- An apple for fractions
- A scale for weight
- A ruler for measurement

Flash cards can be helpful for drilling basic concepts. It is important to note, however, that flash cards should only be used after basic concepts have been learned.

- Numbers 1–100
- Addition and subtraction
- Multiplication and division

Computation and its application, the ability to use numbers and concepts in non-abstract, relevant ways, is the number one neglected area in mathematics. Students need to be able to use their numerical abilities in a variety of ways.

- Rounding to the nearest tenth, hundredth . . .
- Counting by 2's, 3's, 4's . . .
- Coin usage
- Concepts of more than, less than, equal to . . .
- Weather and temperature . . .
- Picture line cards to reinforce awareness of first, last, second, middle and next to middle

Cultural Enrichment

Cultural enrichment activities should aid the child in developing deeper appreciation of his cultural heritage and his place in his culture. Out of cultural enrichment a higher sense of self-esteem should emerge. Low self-esteem is a major factor where children fail in school. African-American children live in a society that too often denigrates blacks. Helping children feel good about themselves is a very special task of those who work with children.

Activities

- Maintain folder on cultural enrichment.
- Write a story about ME.
- Identify the continent of ancestors.
- Cut out pictures from black magazines.
- Make a file on personalities who have succeeded in occupations other than entertainment and sports.
- Write poems about self and others—places and things.
- Write plays about black heroes.
- Learn about a new black hero a month. Discuss various holidays and their meanings.
- Dress up in (African clothing for Kwanzaa) native clothing for special holidays.
- Study great civilizations of Africa.
- Discuss black art posters.
- Look at or read *Ebony, Essence, Black Enterprise* or other ethnic-oriented magazines
- Interact with black or other ethnic toys and books

Social Studies

Social studies activities help students better understand themselves, their environments and other people.

Activities

- Draw pictures of self and family.
- Discuss trips made to specific locations.
- Draw pictures of scenes of field trips.
- Recognize and discuss jobs and skills required.
- Use flannel figures to identify community helpers.
- Locate home, city and state on map.
- Discuss some positive facts of another race or culture.
- Discuss how many cultural groups helped build America.
- Cut out pictures on the way people live in other countries.
- Locate countries on map or globe. Identify the continents where countries are located.
- Identify bodies of water near the countries.

SAMPLE PROGRAM PLAN

Goals:

1. To assist students of grades K–8 with homework assignments, basic learning skills reinforcement, and cultural activities.
2. To help children in learning how to learn, and learning to live and work with others.

Components

1. Academic skills reinforcement at appropriate levels:
   a. Basic mathematics (times tables, fractions, percentages, dividing, subtracting, etc.)
   b. Basic reading (words, definitions, context of words, pronunciation of words, use of nouns, verb/agreements of subject and predicate, etc.)
   c. Basic writing (short stories, essays, letters, notes)—ability to express self appropriately and accurately
   d. Use of resources to accomplish learning
   e. How to use the dictionary (Look It Up)

    f. How to use the encyclopedia

    g. How to use computers

    h. How to use other resources

2. Appreciation and use of learning places
   The community

    1. Library

    2. Museums

    3. Schools

    4. Churches

    5. Parks

    6. Others

3. Cultural heritage

    a. My African heritage

    b. My American heritage

    c. Role models from my heritages

    d. Great events in my people's history

4. Self-exploration

    a. What kind of a person do I want to be?

    b. What does it take for me to get to be that person?

    c. Exercising self-control

    d. How to work toward, and wait for, the PRIZE

    e. Developing my talents

    f. Choosing a worthwhile hobby

(I am an important person only if I will do right things in the right way—my values)

5. Me and others

    a. Getting along with others

    b. Why it is better to think than to fight?

    c. Respect for my parents and authority

    d. Why observing rules and regulations makes life happier.

BEYOND THE SCHOOL SUBJECTS

Certain learnings are so critical in the life of youth—learnings that should begin at home and be reinforced in school—that they may be called *beyond the school subjects*. These subjects include character, values, and morality. More often learned through informal processes, these *subjects* are as important as the planned curriculum courses in school, if no more so.

Given the fluctuating standards of values, morality, and character in today's world, many youth may be confused. Altering home environments and changing family patterns find the home assuming less of the role as *value transmitter.* Many have turned to the schools since this institution historically has placed the development of morality as one of its goals. Today, open discussion of character, morality, and values tend to be bypassed by the school for fear of sanction regarding the separation of church and state.

The after-school program, however, as a community-based service, often housed and cooperating in partnership with a church or other private organization, may take the initiative to build into its *program plan* activities and instruction in the *beyond the school* subjects.

While all youth may profit from planned and structured instruction and activities in the *subjects,* at-risk youth more often will need the experiences. Already at risk due to disruptive factors in the home environment, many youth come to school and the after-school program with attitudes and behavior that have been influenced by *hard* life experiences. Therefore, the messages that the school environment conveys through its routine practices and activities may be missed by the child. The student may consider the messages as *soft* in comparison to his/her past experiences that have been *hard* and ignore them. Carefully planned efforts are required to get the attention of at-risk youth, hold their attention, and engage them emotionally and intellectually in discussions and activities.

Some suggested activities for *beyond the school subjects* learning:

- Utilize one *enrichment* session each week to explore ethics; explore the topics of individual responsibility (relate freedom to responsibility), accentuate the *power of choice;* get youth talking about their beliefs and why they have the beliefs.
- Invite role models to sessions—role models may not always be famous people; local citizens who accomplish, stand out and do good, and especially those who have overcome obstacles.
- Develop projects and activities that require youth to *share;* help youth develop generational appreciation and sensitivity (choose an elderly person[s] to visit, communicate with, help with tasks); encourage sensitivity to the weak, disadvantaged and handicapped. Curwin

(1993) notes that when we help at-risk students, we send the message that they are inferior; when roles are reversed and youth see themselves as being genuinely helpful, they may take pride in themselves.

- Maintain ongoing activities where each student must do his or her part for the effort to succeed. Have students develop guidelines for sanctions on participation.
- Focus attention on *work,* the variety of occupations; help youth become more sophisticated about the world of work—explore the reality of *performing occupations* (major league positions in sports, entertainment) and the number and rate of those who actually become *famous;* help restore appreciation of the *helping professions.*
- Ensure that there is a mechanism for conflict resolution—allow students to help in developing guidelines and in the *negotiations.*
- Involve parents in *beyond school subjects* through sharing activities in the enrichment session and through discussions in the Parent Practica.
- Encourage and create activities for reading beyond school materials; surround youth with positive magazines; have them read articles from time to time and report on the article (articles may include indirect lessons on *real life*).

Daily Schedule for an After-School Learning Center

2:30–3:00 p.m.	Arriving, choosing goals for the afternoon
3:00–3:30 p.m.	Snacks
3:30–4:30 p.m.	Homework, basic skills activities, Daily Word Dolch Reading List, dictionary presentation, GPS activities, use Resources Packages
4:30–5:00 p.m.	Enrichment folders (creative activities—poetry writing, clippings from magazines, African-American history, cultural games), Guest resource persons (Tues.): music, math, languages, etc.
5:00–5:30 p.m.	Put away, prepare to leave

Suggested Time Frames for the 3:30–4:30 session:

Reading	15 minutes
Language Arts	15 minutes
Mathematics	15 minutes
Social Studies	15 minutes

Implementing the Program Plan

One way to implement the *instructional plan* or *program* is to bring children together across age, grade, interest or needs lines. The children, and persons who work with them, may be referred to as the Group (or the place as the table or center). A Group may focus on language arts at a grade level or work at an age level when specific needs associated with that age and learning needs are evidenced. A person who leads the instructional activities may be called the Group Leader. The Group Leader may be joined by volunteer tutors. Paid tutors may be Group Leaders. The Group Leader works under the Lead Tutor who should coordinate the work of the groups and determine where they stand in the instructional activities. The Lead Tutor works under the general supervision of the Site Supervisor.

The Group Leader sees that *resources packages* are available for each of the groups. The packages are kept current with the aid of the Group Leader and members of the "team." The packages may be a file box into which GPS information is kept along with an ample supply of instructional aids to supplement and enhance the Standards.

A sample layout of the **Groups plan** is shown.

TABLE/CENTER ROUTINES DAILY

Have: Dictionaries on Tables (3:30–5 p.m.)
Utilize: Dolch Word Development (3:30–4:30 p.m.)
Focus on: GPS Guidelines (4–5 p.m.)
Use: Prepared Activities Sheet (3:30–4:30 p.m.)
Explore: Cultural Enrichment (4:30–5 p.m.)

DOLCH WORD LIST

The Dolch Word List contains 220 Sight words. These words comprise 75% of the words read by students in elementary grades and 50% of all words ready by adults. Mastery of these words is essential for such exercises as reading a newspaper or magazine.

Words in the list are placed in the order of difficulty. At the appropriate grade and comprehension levels, the words may be utilized in a number of ways. Definitions (use dictionary), parts of speech, verb tenses, synonyms and antonyms, and use in sentences.

It is best to work on one column at a time at a pace that feels comfortable for the learner.

GROUP CENTER/ TABLE	LEADER STAFF/VOLUNTEER		LEADER STAFF/VOLUNTEER
	K - 3 (5 - 9) GRADE AGE FOCUS	*Tutor one-on-one <u>when possible</u>. Combine lessons when necessary; "team work" on concepts.	4 - 5 (10 - 12) GRADE AGE FOCUS

GROUP CENTER/ TABLE	LEADER STAFF/VOLUNTEER		LEADER STAFF/VOLUNTEER
	6 - 7 (12 - 13) GRADE AGE FOCUS	*Tutor one-on-one <u>when possible</u>. Combine lessons when necessary; "team work" on concepts.	7 - 8 (12 - 14) GRADE AGE FOCUS

TABLE/CENTER ROUTINES DAILY

Have: Dictionaries on Tables (3:30 - 5 p.m.)

Utilize: Dolch Word Development (3:30 - 4:30 p.m.)

Focus on: GPS Guidelines (4 - 5 p.m.)

Use: Prepared Activities Sheet (3:30 - 4:30 p.m.)

Explore: Cultural Enrichment (4:30 - 5 p.m.)

A number of games and puzzles may be used for drill and reinforcement activities for Dolch words.

1	2	3	4
a	look	they	am
I	can	that	under
too	good	going	before
to	brown	did	walk
two	six	who	stop

the	be	like	out
in	today	come	his
see	not	had	make
into	little	saw	your
and	one	no	ride
up	black	long	help
blue	my	yes	call
she	at	an	here
yellow	all	three	sleep
he	so	this	cold
go	by	around	will
you	do	was	pretty
we	are	just	them
big	him	ten	when
red	her	get	around
jump	on	if	as
it	green	soon	white
play	eat	its	funny
down	four	some	put
for	said	from	take
old	away	fly	of
is	run	then	say
me		but	
5	6	7	8
or	right	goes	only
ran	why	small	pick
work	please	find	don't
with	upon	could	gave
there	give	fall	every
about	once	think	which
after	together	far	our
what	us	found	want
ask	tell	read	thank
sing	ate	were	better
must	where	best	clean
five	many	because	been
myself	warm	grow	never
over	laugh	fast	those

cut	live	off	write
let	now	draw	first
again	came	bring	these
new	buy	got	both
have	hold	much	own
how	would	does	hurt
keep	hot	show	eight
drink	open	any	wash
sit	light	try	full
made	their	kind	use
went	pull	wish	done
has	may	carry	start
seven		know	

The Dolch Word List was developed by Edward Dolch, as the Dolch Basic Sight Word List. Other word lists have been developed, but Dolch continues to be used in schools and related reading activities and programs.

TUTORS

Tutors provide a major service in direct learning/reinforcement and homework assistance. Tutors should complete a required training program or sessions before they are given assignments. The contents of the training sessions should include discussion of goals and purposes of the program, why tutors are needed and services they perform, techniques in tutoring, and an observation period before actual tutoring begins.

Tutors should work under the supervision of persons identified as staff. A *staff volunteer* is defined in the section on "Human Resources."

There are many good references on tutoring and tutoring techniques and the Center Staff should study them.

The Tutor and the Student

The tutor should:

- Introduce self to student in a relaxed manner. Learn name of student and pronounce it correctly. Learn short forms of name student uses, if any. Tutor writes his/her name for the student.

- Let student know that the tutor is interested in him by asking about his/her interests, friends; mention student's dress, new haircut, etc.
- Give student full attention. Listen to what he has to say.
- Let student know the tutor is human, too. Tutor admits it when mistakes are made.
- Set an example for student by being courteous and respectful.
- Build student's self-confidence. Let student know you expect him to try. (Low self-esteem plagues many after-school program youth.)
- Don't expect student to show appreciation for efforts.
- Use voice well. Speak softly and slowly. Add variety to speech.
- Communicate with Group Leader or Lead Tutor regularly.
- Follow the center's plan for the tutoring session.
- Be prepared: have all materials ready. (The learning packages should be available and the Lead Tutor who may be the Group Leader should assure that tutors are prepared.)
- Look for ways to motivate student by involving him/her in the activities and by being creative and imaginative in the tutoring methods.
- Keep lesson moving. When tutor notices student losing interest, he should consult Group Leader or Lead Tutor about changes.
- If the student doesn't know answers, make sure he/she has time to think, but give the answer before he feels uncomfortable.
- Do not tell student, *This is easy.* He will feel defeated if he fails in the task.
- Show student that reading can be fun for enjoyment.
- Ask Group Leader or Lead Tutor for help when a learning or behavioral problem arises and tutor is not sure how to handle it.
- Share magazines and other illustrative materials that are available in student's culture.
- Talk up heroes and role models of people in student's culture.
- Gently redirect negative statements student may make about self and others like himself.

Additional Notes on Tutoring

- The Lead Tutor should furnish tutor with background information on student(s) and indicate areas of weakness of instruction.
- Tutor should begin tutoring at a level well within the grasp of the student. This will provide an atmosphere of success. Remember,

many students have had little success in school and need a rewarding experience to restore their self-confidence.

- Indicate immediately whether the student's answers are right or wrong. Let him know you are pleased with a right answer. If he is wrong, do not show disapproval but look at the mistake as a challenge.
- Establish a convenient time to meet with the Center Staff at regular intervals to compare notes.
- Depending on the team's plans, tutor could:
  Keep charts of the student's individual progress to promote interest.
  Devise practical problems for the student to solve.

Approaches That Have Proven Valuable

- The less work the tutor does for the student, the better. Although it is quicker, easier and less frustrating for a tutor to do a problem or an assignment, it is of little permanent help to the student. Help student learn *how* to do his own work. A good tutor will spend most of the time asking *questions, listening and helping the student think for himself or herself,* rather than lecturing to the student.
- When an answer is supplied, be sure the student understands how the answer was determined. If not sure that he does, test student with a similar example. In this manner, the student should be able to handle what he is being helped with.
- Move on to more challenging material as soon as a working relationship is established. Once you feel the tutoring is going well, do not be guilty of under-expectation. If you expect little from the student, he will produce little. With encouragement he may come to have high expectations for himself.
- To the extent possible, be creative and imaginative in tutoring methods. Look for ways to motivate student and to involve him or her.

ESTABLISHING GUIDELINES

The after-school center: What it can and cannot do. Parents should be helped to understand how an after-school program works. What are realistic expectations of the center for the child and the parent? Clearly written statements that convey to parents specific meanings and messages are a must.

The Parent Commitment Form and Participant Form along with the

What the Center Can and Cannot Do form help to assure understandings on the part of all persons involved.

A Child Advocacy/Parent Education After-School Enrichment Program

What A Center Can Offer

a. A safe, enriching environment for two and one-half hours after school.
b. Opportunities to use learning materials required in life-long learning (dictionaries, encyclopedias, learning exercises, educational videos, etc.).
c. Guidance from mature, caring adult leaders.
d. Opportunities to undertake instructional exercises that are designed at GP (grade passing) levels.
e. Opportunities to explore special interest and cultural heritage.
f. *Assistance* with homework.
g. At least one and a half hours devoted to cognitive/cultural activities (learning) and self-explorations.
h. Male mentors (Saturday) program.

What a Center May Require

Parent cooperation through:
    Attendance at the *parent practicums*
    Commitment to cooperate with center activities.
    Commitment to assist child for positive behavior
Students cooperation:
    Child comes to center with positive attitudes and self-controlled behavior
    Child respects adult leaders, materials, resources and the center environment
    Child attends regularly

What a Center Can and Cannot Do

- CANNOT guarantee change in child's school progress. The program provides the opportunity—the child must be receptive
- CANNOT provide discipline that should be taught at home.
- CANNOT serve as baby-sitter—children must come with a purpose

- CANNOT maintain child in program if parents refuse to be part of the Parent Practicum
- CAN assist parent through *self-development* facet of program
- CAN help child and parents gain newer levels of awareness
- CAN help in bonding between parent and child
- CAN help child toward more effective school experiences and living

TESTS AND TESTING

The *after-school* program like all good endeavors will be interested in the degree of effectiveness of its program. Funding agencies often require some form of proof that changes have occurred as a result of the use of funds, and parents more often want to know how their children are doing.

While the after-school program expects to measure to some degree the success of the program, the use of testing as a means of assessing how children are doing in the center raises several questions: The student who comes to the after-school program is likely to be *test shy.* The center should pride itself on its more relaxed atmosphere and less stressful environment. There are the considerations as to who would select, administer, evaluate, and follow up on standardized tests. Considering the issues that are associated with *standardized testing,* use in the center is a less desirable option. Follow-ups on positive changes in schoolwork and attitudes are preferred means of assessment.

Parents should be astute about the testing experiences found at school. They should know when the child is taking a test and for what reason. Moreover, they should have conferences with the child's teachers and ask for interpretations of the test scores. Most reputable school districts will make test scores and records available to parents with officials on hand to interpret and explain the scores. Low-income and less sophisticated parents may not know of the Family Educational Rights and Privacy Act of 1974 that mandates that all schools receiving federal aid must make all official student records available to parents (Boskin, 1975). Prior to the passage of this legislation, seeking test results of a child could prove to be a fruitless effort. Cases have been recorded where parents sought the help of after-school personnel to get their children tested because they were not doing well in their grade placement. These parents were concerned that their children were not going to pass the grade, and sought the test results as a device for a defense if the child failed the grade. After counseling with the parents about the pitfalls of testing/placement, they had a better grasp of the larger experience. Instead, they began to work with their children—visiting the classroom, assisting with homework, varying the children's experiences, and encouraging them to reach their higher potentials.

On the other hand, recent news items indicate that some parents are "begging school psychologists to test their children for mental disabilities even though they know their children are not disabled" (Klausnitzer, 1994). "They want their children classified because it's money in the bank," according to school officials. Such behavior by parents is further indication of the dimensions to which child abuse can extend, and the variety of ways that children are at risk.

Some after-school programs are part of a growing *tutoring industry*. Franchises exist in many cities and companies such as Sylvan, The Reading Game, Huntington Learning Centers, and Humanex Systems have large volumes of clients. These companies rely heavily on testing and charge significant fees. These programs, as noted in an earlier section of this work, do not fall into the category of the *community-based after-school* program. There are effective after-school programs that are free or have nominal costs that are associated with colleges and universities, local schools, and nonprofit private agencies that may consider testing activities. When certified staffs are available in the programs and there are specified purposes for utilizing test procedures, it would appear that testing is acceptable. Some *after-school* programs have utilized such inventories of learning styles as Barsch Learning Styles. Parents must give consent for the administration of the tests and the results should be explained to them and to the child. Some *after-school* programs offer clinics in *test-taking skills.* Academic assistance work in the center should be aimed at helping children in basic and specific learnings and skills that should offset *test-shyness* and self-doubt. The work in self-esteem building aids children to better deal with uncertainties.

These tests are among the most important decisions that are made about placing children in different ability groups and determining to some degree the general academic reputation of the student for life.

(Tracking and placement are discussed in the Introduction of this book.)

Some tests that the child is likely to experience include:
Early Years
    Reading readiness

Metropolitan Readiness Test
Lee-Clark Reading Readiness Test
Murphey-Durrell Readiness Test
Primary Years
Utis Lennon Mental Ability Test
California Test of Mental Maturity
Otis Quick Stock Scoring Mental Ability Test
Achievement Tests
Stanford-Binet Achievement Tests
Iowa Test of Basic Skills
Metropolitan Achievement Test
College Entrance Tests
Preliminary Scholastic Aptitude Test (PSAT)
Scholastic Aptitude Test (SAT)
American College Testing Programs, ACT may be used in the
senior year of high school as an alternative to the SAT
National Merit Scholarship requires applicants to take the SAT.

Testing has become a mainstay of the educational scene in the United States according to Sonia Neito (1992) and tests have been found to be culturally biased. Given the power that testing has in America's schools, the testing industry should be closely monitored, evaluated and rigorously challenged. Members of the Association of Black Psychologists have questioned norm-referenced testing and point to the fact that men like Sir Francis Galton, Lewis Terman and Carl Brigham have used interpretations of their research to support theories on the nature of intelligence of non-European groups (Samuda, 1986).

REFERENCES

Blumfeld, S. L. (1974). *How to tutor.* New Rochelle, NY: Arlington House.

Boskin, M. (1975). *A candid handbook for dealing with your child's school.* NY: Walker.

Craig, R. (1991, September/October). Teacher's stories: An attempt at values integration. *Clearing House, 65,* 39–42.

Curwin, R. (1993, November). The healing power of altruism. *Educational Leadership, 5*(3), 36–39.

Day, B. (1988). *Early childhood education. Creative learning activities* (3rd ed.). New York: Macmillan.

Dolch, E. (1936, February). Basic Sight Vocabulary. *Elementary School Journal, 36,* 456–60.

Ehly, S. W., & Larsen, S. C. (1990). *Peer tutoring for individualized instruction.* Boston: Allyn and Bacon.

Ellis, K., Cogan, J., & Howey, K. (1986). *Introductions to the foundations of education* (2nd ed.). Englewood Cliffs, NJ: Prentice-Hall.

Golick, M. (1987). *Playing with words.* Portsmouth, NH: Heinemann.

Goodlad, J. I. (1984). *A place called school: Prospects for the future.* New York: McGraw-Hill.

Goodman, J. & Hammil, D. (1975). *Basic schools skills inventory.* Chicago: Follett.

Hansen, J. (1993, December). Teaching life concerns to kids who don't care. *NAASP Bulletin, 77,* 46–50.

Henson, T. (1988). *Methods and strategies for teaching in secondary and middle schools.* New York: Longmans.

Hill, M. (1989). *Home. Where reading and writing begin.* Portsmouth, NH: Heinemann.

Katz, L., & Shard, S. (1989). *Engaging children's minds. The Project approach.* Norwood, NJ: Ablex.

Klausnitzer, D. (1994, June 26). Parents attempt to cash-in. Nashville, *The Tennessean,* 1–2A.

Lederman, E. (1987). *Educational toys and games.* Springfield, IL: Charles C Thomas, Publisher.

Leming, J. (1993, November) In search of effective character education (synthesis of research). *Educational Leadership, 51*(3), 63–71.

Likona, T. (1993, November). The return of character education. *Educational Leadership, 51*(3), 6–11.

Maeroff, G. (1989). *School-smart parent. A guide to knowing what you should know — From infancy through elementary school.* New York: Times Books.

National Commission on Excellence in Education. (1983). *A nation at risk. The imperative for educational reform.* Washington, DC: Government Printing Office.

National Education Association. Commission on the Reorganization of Secondary Education. (1918). *Cardinal principles of secondary education.* The Association.

Nieto, S. (1992). *Affirming diversity. The sociopolitical context of multicultural education.* New York: Longmans.

Phillips, D. C., & Soltis, J. F. (1985). *Perspectives on learning.* New York: Teachers College, Columbia University.

Portelli, J. P. (1984, Summer). On defining curriculum. *Journal of Curriculum and Supervision, 2*(4), 354–67.

Samuda, R. (Ed.) & Shies, K. (1986). *Multicultural education programs and methods.* Toronto: Intellectual Social Science Publications.

Schaefer, E. S. (1969). A home tutoring program. *Children, 16*(2), 59–61.

Swanson, M. (1991). *At-risk students in elementary education. Effective schools for disadvantaged learners.* Springfield, IL: Charles C Thomas, Publisher.

Taylor, D., & Strickland, D. (1986). *Family storybook reading.* Portsmouth, NH: Heinemann.

Thayer, L. (1981). *Fifty strategies for experiential learning. Book two.* San Diego, CA: University Associates, Inc.

Thomas, G. & Roberts, C. (1994, May). The character of our schooling. *American School Board Journal, 18*(5) 33–36.

Topping, K. (1989). Peer tutoring and paired reading: Combining two powerful techniques. *The Reading Teacher, 42,* 488–494.

——. (1987). *The peer tutoring handbook: Promoting cooperative learning.* Cambridge, MA: Brookline Books.

Tyler, R. W. (1949). *Basic principles of curriculum and instruction.* Chicago: University of Chicago Press.

Vail, E. (1967) *Tools of teaching: Techniques for stubborn cases of reading, spelling and behavior.* Springfield, IL: Charles C Thomas, Publisher.

Walberg, H. et al. (1985, April). Homework's power effects on learning. *Educational Leadership,* 76–79.

Part III

THE PARENT FOCUS

The family is the major institution that influences the development of the child. When children are in need of help, more often their families also need help. Therefore, it is aptly said that *work with children without work with parents is work half done.*

The need for work with parents is validated by several factors:

- Children learn more when parents and teachers work together.
- Most parents would like to be more active in their children's school experiences but don't know how to begin.
- Many parents have to be helped before they can realize that they can assist their children in their schooling.
- Parents are natural advocates for their children, but many must be helped in assuming this role.
- Parents who help their children in their educational activities also help to improve themselves.

Parents are the child's first teacher, whether they want the role or not. It is from the parent or parents—surrogate parent or caregiver—that the child discovers who he or she is, or the *self-concept.* Parental influence continues throughout the child's years of growth and development but lessens when peer influences intervene. The effectiveness of earlier parent guidance and training may well influence the extent and the degree that peer pressure influences the child.

Parents and their degree of interest and participation in their children's schooling vary. Some educators and parent educators have described the following types of parents that have been observed among the parents of children enrolled in after-school programs:

1. Parents who express interest in their children's education and are actively involved in volunteer activities at the school and in helping their children with homework and related school assignments. These parents visit the school regularly, ask questions about lessons and the curriculum, and seek out teachers for conferences.

2. Parents who are interested but make no effort to be involved. These parents may be from a cultural orientation that believes the school knows best and accepts whatever the school does.

3. Parents who are interested in their children but for some reason, perhaps simple neglect or other concerns, find it difficult to express their interests.

4. Parents who do not express interest and have no involvement because of a general suspicion of schools and persons in positions of authority. These parents may harbor resentment from previous experiences with the schools as a student or a parent.

5. Parents who may be like #4 and harbor resentment of schools, perhaps having been a school dropout, and for other reasons. These parents are likely to be resentful of authority and of friends who may still be in school and appear to be succeeding. These feelings of hostility and resentment may be transmitted to the child. Teenage parents often fit the mold.

WORKING WITH PARENTS

When the parent registers the child in the after-school program (parents should be urged to register the child as opposed to another person), the initial conference is held. This meeting is the occasion for the Parent Educator (PE) to meet the parent and the child that should accompany the parent. From the beginning, the PE, like any human being, will have **first impressions** of the parent. It is at this point and throughout the relationship that the staff must consider and maintain objective attitudes and demonstrate positive behaviors no matter what the circumstances. Many forces, internal and external, influence the way parents think and behave:

1. No two parents are alike. The mother and father of a child may differ in their viewpoints and attitudes. Staff must resist the temptation to look for a *model parent.*

2. Parents' attitudes and spirit of cooperation may be influenced by factors that are not readily visible. Poor housing, ill health, worry over inadequate income, marital, and social problems can alter attitudes. The after-school staff member gets to know the child and his parents and the conditions that may influence their participation and attitudes.

3. Parents must be respected and their viewpoints taken into consideration. Many parents have strong convictions about the things they do and why they do them. They feel that they know more about their child and may be reluctant to give up their positions. Patience and flexibility as well as willingness to listen and negotiate are required.

4. Parent education is said to be yet another dimension of *multicultural education.* Parents' responses to children and the schools may have origins in cultural/ethnic histories of the family. Parents may have differing ways of expressing interest and differing expectations of the child and the school. Some socioeconomic groups believe girls waste their time in school, and being taught by a female is *unmanly* for a male. Appreciation of diversity is required.

5. Survival is the priority of parents, and for some it is difficult to accept the time spent in school as having real meaning. Therefore, when parents allow their children to *miss school* to earn wages, the staff must be objective in its responses and seek to understand all the variables that may exist.

6. Willingness to listen to parents and to observe their needs and states of life; willingness to negotiate and the development of flexibility in time and attitude are essential.

7. Willingness to answer questions and to encourage questions are necessary. Through questions and answers much learning can take place, both for the educator and the parent.

Sensitive vs. Insensitive Attitudes and Values in Working with Parents

SENSITIVE	INSENSITIVE
Do with	Do for
Work alongside	Lead
Assist	Control
Provide input	Advise
Facilitate	Determine
Provide additional resources	Impose additional requirements
Encourage	Mandate
Respect	Condescend
Display concern	Display maternalism/paternalism
Demonstrate empathy	Demonstrate sympathy

The Interview

The interview and the conference are two experiences during which time the after-school staff member or members have one-on-one communication with the child's parent(s). The interview is generally the initial meeting of the parent, child and member of the after-school staff. This meeting is usually held during the time the child is registered in the program. The purposes of the interview include eliciting information from the parent on vital data about the child and the perceptions of the parent(s) as to the needs of the child.

The conference may be a staff-initiated experience where the staff member spends time explaining the center's activities, goals and objectives, specific lessons, and the child's progress or lack of it in relation to the program. The parent also participates in the conferences in raising questions and seeking answers about the child's day-to-day performances. Parents may request a conference with a staff member at any time.

The interview may be accompanied by a questionnaire that seeks such information as to the child's relationship with the parents, siblings, and other residents in the home, and the child's schedule from day to day (when he or she gets up, goes to bed, home chores, homework time, play time, recreation and meals, etc.). During the first or subsequent meetings, the staff member should get to know the opinions of the parent(s) about the child's education—is it seen as an imperative in the life of the child, or simply a requirement; what are the hopes of the parent(s) for the future of the child; what are the expectations of the after-school program; if the parents are willing to participate in the "Parent Practicum" and if they are willing to help the child in his educational experiences; what are specific concerns the parent(s) have about the child, and if the parent(s) are willing to become involved (volunteer) in the center experiences affecting their child and other children.

The questionnaire completed from the interview and notes from conferences should be maintained in a folder containing basic data about the child. Study of these materials should aid the staff in better serving the individual child.

Sample interview form   DATE: _____

NAME _____

PARENT OF _____

1. (Please place an X by one of the following:)

__ My child is improving because of the program
__ My child is not improving

2. I have some recommendations. (Please write them on the back of this sheet.)
3. The Practicum (Please place an X by one of the following:)
__ Have been helpful
__ Have not been helpful

4. Why have they not been helpful if you checked *have not been?* (Please explain on the back of this sheet.)
5. (Please place an X by one of the following:)
__ I enjoy the parent group
__ I do not enjoy the parent group
(Please explain your response on the back of this sheet.)

6. (Please place an X by one of the following:)
I need more help with my child
__ Yes   __ No

7. (Please place an X by one of the following:)
Overall, the Program is
__ Meeting my child's needs
__ Not meeting my child's needs
(Please explain your response on back of this sheet.)

8. I think the Program's strengths are
9. I think the Program's weaknesses are

Home Visits

The center program decides if visits to the child's home will be among the services. The *home visits* should have a specific purpose and fit into the overall plan of the program. Visiting with parents in the home in order to provide families and children the service and support they need represents the ultimate expression of what the helping profession is all about (Morrison, 1978).

The after-school program is more likely to establish home visits for the purposes of interviews, conferences, and training sessions with parent and child. The parent focus may include the *parent trainer* as a staff member who works under the supervision of the Parent Educator (PE) and visits homes to demonstrate ways of using learning resources and how the home environment may be used as a source for facilitating learning.

In considering home visits, several factors should be kept in mind: (a) establish rapport with parent before planning a home visit; (b) have a specific goal in mind for the visit; (c) prepare for the interview, conference, *lesson* or experience; (d) advise the parent as to the nature of the visit; (e) visit the home with an open mind (avoid being judgmental); and (f) get to know the community before visiting the home.

Records

Files and records are essential to the coordination and continuity of an efficient service (McLoughlin, 1987). Educators and persons that work in educational settings have a responsibility to document contacts with families and progress of each child in its program. Each child should have a folder containing basic identifying information, health needs, and who to contact in case of an emergency. The child's school status should be on file as well as samples of his work and notations of his progress.

The parent and child *commitment* forms should be in the child/parent(s) registration folder. The parent(s)' file should contain identifying data, notes from the parent and copies of communications sent and received; parent(s)' participation in the Practica and other activities such as membership in the parent group and volunteer activities.

LEVELS OF PARENT PARTICIPATION

The process of enrolling a child or children in the center program is one level of commitment. The minimum involvement the program may require includes attendance at the Parent Practica, a series of four to five seminars or workshops held each year by the center program and coordinated by the Parent Educator, center staff and resource persons. The program may also require parents to participate in parent/tutor conferences. Conferences should be held periodically to share information with parents on the progress of the child. The conference should elicit suggestions to get insights from parents and assess parents' views of the program's effectiveness.

Another level of parent involvement is that of the *parent partnership*. Partnership is defined as full sharing of skills, knowledge and experiences in helping children in their educational experiences and develop-nt. The *parent as a partner* undoubtedly assumes greater responsibilities in the work of the after-school program. The single most appropriate word for the *partnership* is *sharing*. Much of the sharing involves knowl-edge by the parent in relating experiences the parent has had with his/her child. The experiences and the accompanying learnings the parent gains are invaluable as the PE and staff seek to know and serve the child and his parent. The PE and staff in turn share knowledge with the parent. Knowledge is shared through conferences, workshops/seminars (the Practica), home visits and in the parent-tutor setting.

The active participation of the parent as a partner should include levels of decision making. The parent makes recommendations and seeks to have opinions, ideas, and observations considered and appropri-ately absorbed into the *program plan*. The partner who assumes this level should have demonstrated *participation* at a level well above the initial and prescribed *involvement/commitment*. Parents who enter into the decision-making experience should have participated in the program's activities as "tutor," member of committees, participant in the group's programs and the Practica.

With appropriate background and preparation, the parent partner can participate in home visits and training of other parents, overseeing learning materials collections, assisting in planning budgets, initiating fund-raising projects, and in sharing in formulating and setting goals and objectives.

Success of the *parent partnership* lies in mutual respect. The center staff respect the parent; the parent respects the center staff and its program. Working as a team, parents and staff can do remarkable things for the center's program and the children served.

The Parent Practica

The Parent Practica is the parent education/training course, workshop, or seminar that is designed as part of the after-school program service to parents. It may choose as its goals to bring together parents of children in the center for the purpose of sharing information on parenting, encour-aging parents' participation in their children's education, and assisting parents in becoming advocates for their children in school and life.

Parents are expected to attend and participate in the **practica**. Upon registration of the child in the center program the parent should sign the *commitment contract* indicating that the parent understands the purposes and meanings of the *contract* and how fulfilling the terms will help both parent and child.

The practica may be designed around a theme for a year with individual sessions focusing on specific topics. A survey of interests and needs of parents, issues that the staff see as emerging from work with parents and their children, suggestions from other personnel that work with children, and larger societal issues may form the basis for selecting the practica themes from time to time. In planning a recent practica, an after-school program drew upon observations and interviews with parents. Some parents in the center expressed and demonstrated a significant lack of security in their roles as parents. Some felt incapable of being a parent to the point that they sought other persons to assume the care and responsibility of the child. Thus, a practicum was held on *Parent as Person* —what it means to be a parent, duties and responsibilities of a parent, how the parent influences the child in ways no other person can; overcoming insecurities; getting hold of ME, the person; explorations into self, etc.

Complaints conveyed by parents to the after-school staff indicated that most parents had subtle fears of the school, saw it as the adversary, and translated many local values and ways of doing things into expectations from the schools. Many of the fears and resentments were well placed. Parents cited instances of being ignored, treated rudely, and *talked down to* during conferences. A session of the practica was planned to focus on *How the Schools Work.*

A neutral party was identified to conduct this session. The person was knowledgeable about school structure, local school policies, and even aspects of the *hidden curriculum* unique to the local community. Parents were walked, as it were, through public education from the federal to the local level. It was explained how and why schools were organized as they are. The local school's handbook on policies and procedures was examined and discussed. Parents were shown visuals that indicated the differences between the potential earnings and quality of life of youth who complete high school and go on to college as opposed to those who do not. Parents were counseled on the *reality* of the school setting. They were shown how to expect and demand respect from their children's teachers. Their rights and responsibilities as parents, and how to be an effective advocate for their children, were also explored.

A third session dealt with *How Children Learn* and a fourth one focused on *Helping Your Child Succeed in School.*

The practica by whatever name should be an integral part of the after-school program. Work with children without work with their parents is work only half done. It is desirable for the after-school staff in cooperation with a number of other resource persons to design the series of parent seminars/workshops. By so doing the center program is more likely to succeed in making the most appropriate match between local need and service delivery.

In addition to the practica, the parents may want to form a parent group. The parent group may choose to identify a commercial parent education/training course or program for its activities. It may also choose to design its own *program* using a number of *models* as subjects for study.

After School Tutorial/Enrichment Program

Participant Contract

I am interested in the After-School Program and I would like to enroll. I understand and will observe the rules for conduct in the Program. I understand that if I fail to observe the rules, I may not continue in the Program.

1. I will attend regularly unless there are valid reasons for my absences. I will notify the Site Supervisor when I plan to be absent for more than one day.
2. I will cooperate with other children and respect their rights.
3. I will avoid fights and disruptive behavior.
4. I will respect the staff in charge and follow directions.
5. I will avoid being deliberately loud, hitting, and running inside.
6. I will keep in mind that I am in the Program to learn and enjoy enrichment activities.
7. I will take care of things that I use: materials, chairs, etc.
8. I will remain at the Center for at least two hours. I understand that this is a Program with a stable environment.

My parents and I have read this Contract and understand it. If I am too young to understand it, my parent(s), guardian, and/or the Site Supervisor will explain it to me. THE CENTER WANTS TO HELP ME. I MUST COOPERATE BY HELPING MYSELF.

Age of student _____   Student

_____

Address of student _____   Parent or Guardian

_____   Date _____

_____   _____

School Attended   Parent or Guardian

_____   Date _____

Name of Homeroom Teacher

Parent Conferences

The initial conference between the center staff and the parent is likely to be during registration of the child in the after-school program. This process may be called the interview as well.

Parent and teacher or tutor (staff) conferences should be a meeting between the PE or other staff member for the purposes of sharing information about the child. Conferences should be scheduled at such times as are required. Periodic conferences should be scheduled to keep the parent up-to-date. In preparing for the conference the staff person should keep in mind that *teacher/parent* conferences often have built-in potentials for tension. Parents tend to shy away from contact with teachers. Each tends to expect the other to react negatively. The after-school program proposes to assure parents of its advocacy role—to advise and inform as well as to aid in empowering the parent for further advocacy activities.

Developing confidence and a sense of trust between parent and the staff is a major goal. Many parents of children who come to the after-school centers have experienced negative situations with the public schools. Parents of poor children are often labeled as *losers,* and the *at-risk* label tends to single them out—both parent and child. Many years ago, Goethe (1749–1832) said: *If you treat an individual as he is, he will stay as he is, but if you treat him as if he were what he ought to be, and could be, he will become what he ought to be and what he could be.*

In preparing for the parent conference, some common sense rules may be followed:

- Time and Place. The time and place of the conference should be mutually agreed upon. The setting should be comfortable and inviting. The parent may choose the place, however, and the staff member would have no control over it. However, when the staff chooses the place, it should be a setting with maximum effect.

- Notes should be made and followed; list all points that are to be made in the conference.
- Be prepared to adjust the agenda, if need be.
- Initiate the conference with positive and favorable remarks. Be sincere in the remarks; artificiality is readily discerned.
- Give specific examples of the child's performances.
- Be specific and honest about the child's behavior, attitudes and habits.
- Avoid ambiguities and vague examples.
- Employ language that is clear and at an appropriate level for the parent; avoid trying to impress the parent with professional jargon.
- Plan for follow-up conferences and set tentative dates if feasible.

The conference should allow the parent the freedom to express interests and concerns and to get clarifications, explanations, and information from the staff person. The skilled staff member can utilize the conference to advise the parent of the progress or lack of it on the part of the child, but it also provides opportunities to share additional information and literature that can help the parent in a variety of ways.

SAMPLE:

Parent Practica

THEME: Parent as Person

PLACE: The After-School Center

DATE: Open

TIME: 7:00 p.m. to 8:30 p.m.

PRESENTERS: Psychologists, family life counselors

PARTICIPANTS: Parents

OBJECTIVE: To involve parents of children enrolled in the center in critical thinking about their roles as parents and to aid them in coming into new understandings of the roles.

To introduce parents to a series of questions aimed to provoke thinking about self-value, self-awareness, parenting and parenting responsibilities: What is a parent? Why am I a parent? What kind of parent do I want to be? What will it take for me to be the kind of parent I want to be? What do I think of myself? My children? etc.

OUTCOMES: Parents begin to examine self in relation to their children; parents begin to explore alternative ways in doing things and in responding to child(ren) and life circumstances.

THEME: Homework—Parent and Child

PLACE: The After-School Center

DATE: Open

TIME: 7:00 p.m. to 8:30 p.m.

PRESENTERS: Center Staff/Resource Person(s)

PARTICIPANTS: Parents and Child(ren)

OBJECTIVE: To demonstrate and provide practice for parents in homework assistance for the child.

A workshop that gives examples of how homework assistance may be approached; time and place to undertake homework; materials needed in homework experience (dictionary, textbook, etc.). Do's and don'ts in homework assistance. When to ask for help; communicating with the school and the Center. Role-playing activities (parent/child exchange roles)—homework assistance—a learning tool for parent and child.

THEME: How Children Learn

PLACE: The After-School Center

DATE: Open

TIME: 7:00 p.m. to 8:30 p.m.

PRESENTERS: Educational psychologist, child development specialist

PARTICIPANTS: Parents

OBJECTIVE: To aid parents in understanding how children learn.

Discussion on left brain and its functions; the right brain and its functions. The ways (styles) children learn. Discussion on how the parent learns. Different materials and activities to encourage learning.

The Parent Group

The Parent Practica is required of parents as a level of commitment to the child in the center and the program that is offered. Parents and/or PE and other center staff may sense the need for parent training experiences beyond the level of the Practica and initiate efforts to organize parents into a support or other type of group. Parents themselves may perceive the need for a parent group and initiate such a group on their own.

Four distinguishing characteristics should be reflected in the organizational efforts: (a) a core group of parents who are brought or come together with some common interests and goals in mind; (b) a series of meetings held over a period of time; (c) exchanged and shared ideas and experiences; and (d) information sharing (from materials and human resources) to assist parent(s) in definable areas of interest and need.

The activities of the *group* are likely to include: support of the after-school program through a variety of means such as volunteering, fund raising, public relations, etc.; support and networking through contact with other parenting groups; collecting, exchanging and providing information on parenting procedures, and study of the local school system.

When parent groups organize, they generally follow standard parliamentary procedures in determining the internal structure of the organization including selection of officers and conduct of the meetings. Regular meetings may be held wherein the business of the group is conducted. Along with the group's meetings or in a separate event, speakers may be invited to address the group from time to time on topics that are of interest to the group. The group may also use its own membership as a resource in exploration of topics. Methods and procedures in exploring topics and involving all members may include brainstorming, role playing, and interactive panel discussions. When the group chooses topics for discussion as the highlight of any meeting, whether separate or combined, several things should occur:

- Consensus must be arrived at in choosing the topic.
- Everyone that desires to should have the opportunity to speak at least once during the topic discussion.
- All opinions should be valued. No person should be *put down.*
- Discussion leader should see to it that discussions are focused and that getting off on to tangents is avoided.
- Summary of outcomes of the discussions should be prepared as a conclusion.

While the center staff develops the Practica sessions, the parent group will make the decision as regards the ways the group's goals are to be accomplished. In satisfying the need to share information on parenting procedures and practices, the group may develop its own program or choose to follow a commercial parent *training program.* Although the group may not choose a commercial program, it will want to be familiar with a variety of programs, some of which are *models* that have been developed by public and private agencies. The programs represent a wide range of approaches and philosophies. Some parts or sections of several programs may be considered as well as adapting an entire program or concept.

What Individual Parents Are Expected To Do:

1. Attend and participate in the program practica.
2. Help child with homework on a regular schedule.
3. Develop plans to use the PARENT/CHILD CARING/SHARING OUTLINE for *at home and beyond* learning experiences.
4. Make special efforts to learn more about the child's school and its operations. These efforts include seeking and knowing: (a) Child's teachers and principal; school superintendent—office location and telephone number; (b) name of school board representative for the district in which child lives; (c) curriculum type (general, vocational, etc.); (d) testing procedures—how child is placed in grades, homeroom, and seating arrangements in classes; (e) file on child's placement and test scores—grading system for district, school and individual teachers; (f) school handbook stating rules and regulations.
5. Visit school periodically; ask for and secure periodic teacher conferences (do not be discouraged if teacher is not anxious to meet

with you, INSIST; if no success, approach the next level of authority).
6. Know what clubs and organizations exist on the school campus; get to know the numbers of diverse students in these organizations.
7. Participate in PARENT TEACHER ASSOCIATION at the school.

The Parent Educator helps parents with new learnings and knowledge about how to be an effective advocate for the child in school and how to aid the child in getting the most out of the schooling experience.

What the Parent Group Can Do for the Program:
1. Identify successful parents and ask them to share their experiences with parents of children in the center.
2. Invite professionals in areas of specialties to speak to parents at regular or special meetings.
3. Share in fund-raising activities.
4. Provide snacks for children.
5. Volunteer as tutor and in other volunteer activities.
6. Form study groups to explore local school curriculum, textbooks, policies and procedures that affect children.
7. Donate items to the center.
8. Plan and carry out field trips for children.
9. Plan and/or assist with special holiday activities.
10. Serve as resource person (if member parent has an area specialty).
11. Undertake any of the activities listed for *volunteers.*
12. Others as desired and required.

Parent Involvement Form

Commitment Contract

Date _____

Name (Parent or Guardian) _____

                    Last   First   Middle Init.

Address _____

      Number   Apt.   Street   Zip Code

Telephone (Home) _____ (Work) _____

Age Range (Under 18) _____ (Over 18) _____ (Over 55) _____

Male _____ Female _____

    Name of Child _____

    Address _____

(If other than Parent or Guardian)

Child's school grade _____

School attended _____

Special Needs (Physical) Please explain _____

Educational (Please explain) _____

_____

Parent's special interests or desires for the child:

_____

Child's talents or special abilities _____

_____

Transportation: How will the child get to and from the Center?

_____

If someone is designated to call for the child, please give the name and contact number _____

Emergency: In case of an emergency, who should be contacted?

Name and Contact _____

Physician _____

TO THE PARENT: The Center welcomes your child. We want to be partners with you in the development of your child. Helping you help him or her to be happy in school and society and to get the most from the school and have successful experiences is what we are about.

The success of our work with your child will depend a great deal upon your sharing with us in this great adventure.

Please check below if you are willing to:

a. Serve as a volunteer in the Center on occasions _____

b. Assist with field trips on occasions _____

c. Attend parent meetings when possible _____

As a parent of a child in the Center, I promise to attend the Parent Practica sessions, cooperate with staff in interviews, conferences and meetings, and to use the information I get from the various exchanges in helping my child succeed in school and life.

_____

Signed

YOUR CHILD'S DAILY SCHEDULE

A.M.   HOUR

Gets up _____

School _____ to _____

P.M.

Home _____

Study time _____ to _____

Play time _____ to _____

Hobbies/Crafts

    Time _____ to _____

Places to go

    Church _____ to _____

After School _____ to _____

Other _____ to _____

Television _____ to _____

Bed _____

SOME PARENT EDUCATION PROGRAMS— INFORMATION SOURCES

ACTIVE PARENTING offers a six-session course covering a range of topics. It also trains parent educators and others. It is located at 2996 Grandview Avenue, Suite 312, Atlanta, GA 30306.

APPALACHIAN EDUCATIONAL LABORATORY DIVISION OF CHILDHOOD AND PARENTING. Has produced: "It's Never Too Late," "Home Visitors Kit," "Day Care and Home Learning Activities Plan." Address: P.O. Box 13418, Charleston, WV 25325.

ASSOCIATION FOR SUPERVISION AND CURRICULUM DEVELOPMENT offers the *Involving Parents in Education,* a program that includes a thirty-minute video and a 54-page Leader's Guide. It covers such topics as *help parents at parenting, increase parent's volunteer support,* and *involve parents in policy-making.* Located at 250 N. Pitt Street, Alexandria, VA 23314-1453.

CENTER FOR THE IMPROVEMENT OF CHILD CARING is an active parenting program organization that offers parents training and certification of parent trainers. Includes a program called Black Parenting. CICC is located at 11331 Ventura Boulevard, Suite 103, Studio City, CA 91604.

EVEN START FAMILY LITERACY PROGRAM is Part B of Chapter 1, Title I of the Elementary and Secondary Education Act of 1965. Includes provision requiring family participation in three Even Start components: early childhood education, adult literacy, and parenting education. Even Start programs are active throughout school systems in the nation.

EXCEL, INC. THE 4MAT SYSTEM: **Understanding Ourselves-Understanding Our Children,** is a seminar for parents. It offers a slide-tape program designed to help parents better understand that children have differing styles in learning and how they may help the child in the most appropriate and productive ways.

THE FAMILY MATTERS PROJECT AT CORNELL UNIVERSITY has developed a series of research-based training materials for parents, educators, and helping professionals. The project is located at 7 Research Park, Cornell University, Ithaca, NY 14850.

THE FAMILY RESOURCE COALITION, a national grassroots federation of individuals and organizations, promotes the development of prevention-oriented community-based programs and has among its goals to help family resource programs become better advocates for children and families in their states. It produces two guides: Sharing Resources, An Annotated Bibliography of Technical Assistance Materials, and Programs to Strengthen Families—A Resource Guide. FRC is located at 230 N. Michigan Avenue, Suite 1625, Chicago, IL 60601.

HIGH/SCOPE EDUCATIONAL RESEARCH FOUNDATION. Family Programs Department engages in curriculum development, workshops, and seminars for teachers and parent education projects. Located at 600 N. River Street, Ypsilanti, MI 78197.

HOME START DEMONSTRATION PROGRAM was initiated in 1972 as a Head Start demonstration project of the Office of Child Development, Department of Health, Education and Welfare, Washington, D.C. Services are delivered to children through the parent as focal person.

MOTHER–CHILD HOME PROGRAM (MCHP) was initiated in 1965 and directed by Doctor Phyllis Levenstein and sponsored by the Family Services Association of Nassau County, New York for the State University of New York at Stony Brook. The goal of the program is to prevent educational disadvantages in young children.

MOTHEREAD (see After-School Programs).

NATIONAL CONGRESS OF PARENTS AND TEACHERS is organized on local, state, and national levels. Its main functions are advocacy, service and parent education. Located at 700 N. Rush Street, Chicago, IL 60601.

PARENT EFFECTIVENESS TRAINING (PET) is considered by some as the most popular parent training program. It was originated by Thomas Gordon in 1970 in the book, *Parent Effectiveness Training.* A PET course has a leader who models the skills, supervises role play, gives feedback, manages the dynamics, and assigns written exercises. PET is aimed at preventative rather than curative. PET programs are held at a number of sites.

PARENT TRAINING of the Illinois Department of Children and Family Services has produced a 133-page manual on parenting skills training for children *at risk,* abused or neglected. Located at 1 North Old State Capital Plaza, Springfield, IL 62706.

OUTLINE FOR PARENT/CHILD CARING, SHARING AND LEARNING

It is about—

- Parent/Child bonding
- Increasing the effectiveness of parenting
- Strengthening family ties
- Preparing youth for productive, successful living
- Enhancing learning

Excerpts from the
SUMMER SHARING BOOK
for the younger child
JUNE, JULY, AUGUST
FUN THINGS TO DO IN THE SUMMER MONTHS

Sunday

- Attend church or other place of worship with your child.
- Let child *help* with lunch.
- Ask child to tell you something about what happened at church *first, second, third.*
- Read a story. Ask your child what happened *first, second, third.*
- Let child set the table, matching plates with forks and spoons.
- While going on a ride, ask child what would he/she do if he/she got lost.

Monday

- Have your child look at the calendar and name the days of the week and say what month it is.
- Let your child make jello with your directions and help discuss terms: stir, bowl, mix, measuring.
- Have your child stand in *front* and *back* of various objects.
- Have child hop on *left* foot, balance on *right* foot.

Tuesday

- Have child skip, hop; take 3 steps *forward,* 2 steps *backward.*
- Have your child sort buttons or beads by *color,* put them in egg cartons, tell the color.
- Have your child find *letters of the alphabet* on boxes, cans, and other containers.
- Have child trace letters of the alphabet (see work sheet).
- Have your child put the cover on the *top* of the pan; put the pan on *top* of the table.
- Using the newspaper, ask your child to look for *letters* in his/her name.

Wednesday

- Visit local library; check out some books.
- Read a book to your child.
- Let child pick out letters in the book.
- Play rhyming word game: bag—tag, run—fun, etc.
- Start a *scrapbook.* Have child cut pictures identifying colors, objects, activities.
- Count the chairs at dining table. How many are there?
- Use old magazines—cut out pictures of healthy foods.

Thursday

- Let child *help* parent in the kitchen. *Identify* letters on boxes or cans of foods.
- Take child outside and find *house number.*
- *Help* child learn his/her *address.*
- Have child memorize his/her telephone number and 911.
- Show your child a picture for a few seconds. Take away picture and ask child to name as many things he saw as possible.
- Cut out picture from old magazines and select only those of one color for the *scrapbook.*
- *Read* a story to your child at bedtime.

Friday

- Prepare a *food* and ask child to talk about it: taste, color, texture (recipes in this Part).
- Discuss foods—learn about other people and some *customs* they carry out on Friday.
- Watch your child *print* his/her name. Remember to begin name with a capital letter—then lowercase. Example: Mary.
- Examine newspaper. Point out weekend *activities* that are announced in certain sections of some newspapers.
- *Go* to one or more *free events* (art shows, music concerts in the park, etc.) on the weekend or the following week.
- Put date of the event on the calendar.

Saturday

- If you *shop* on this day, let child see *prices* and explain why certain items were chosen.
- Have child trace numbers (see work sheet).
- Give child grocery receipt. Have him/her circle the 5's.
- Ask child what letters certain foods begin with (Example: "p" for potato).
- If Saturday is *cleaning day,* let child *help* with chores.
- Point out *letters* on cleaning materials containers.
- Have child identify the numbers in the *prices* on the shelf labels at stores.
- Play guessing game. Example: Say, "I'm thinking of a color. What is it?"

Using a calendar for each month, schedule one or more activities to do each day of the week.

Parent/Child
Activities and Recipes

Finger Play

Where is *Thumbkin?* (Repeat all lines 3 times)
Here I am.
How are you this morning?
Very well, I thank you.
(Run and hide)

Where is *Pointer?* (Repeat all lines 3 times)
Here I am.

How are you this morning?
Very well, I thank you.
(Run and hide)

Where is *Middle* finger? (Repeat all lines 3 times)
Here I am.
How are you this morning?
Very well, I thank you.
(Run and hide)

Where is *Ring finger?* (Repeat 3 times)
Here I am.
How are you this morning?
Very well, I thank you.
(Run and hide)

Where is *Pinkie?* (Repeat 3 times)
Here I am.
How are you this morning?
Very well, I thank you.
(Run and hide)

Where is the *Whole Family?* (Repeat 3 times)
Here we are.
How are you this morning?
Very well, I thank you.
(Run and hide)

Songs

"Ten Little Indians"
"Deep and Wide"
"If You're Happy and You Know It"
"I'm Feasting At His Banquet Table"
"Running Over"
"Jesus Loves Me"
"I'm a Little Duck"
"Sunbeam for Jesus"
"Zacchaeus"

Nursery Rhymes

"Humpty Dumpty"

"Little Miss Muffet"
"Little Bo Peep"
"The Cat and The Fiddle"
"Baa Baa Black Sheep"
"Wee Willie Winkie"
"Mary Mary Quite Contrary"

RECIPES

Play Dough

Mix 2 cups flour
1 cup salt
2 teaspoons cooking oil
Water as needed (1/2 cup)
Knead together, store in covered plastic container

Butter

Put a small carton of whipping cream into a jar and shake until butter forms.

Finger Paint Recipe #1

Mix together 1 cup liquid starch, food coloring, and Ivory Flakes.

Finger Paint Recipe #2

Use non-menthol shaving cream and food coloring.

Finger Paint Recipe #3

Mix 2 cups flour and 2 teaspoons salt together.
Add 3 cups cold water and stir.
Add 2 cups hot water and boil until glossy.
Add food coloring or tempera (powdered) paint, let cool.

Peanut Butter Play Dough

This play dough is edible.
2 cups powdered dry milk
2 cups smooth peanut butter
1 cup honey
Mix the ingredients together until it forms a soft, pliable, good-tasting modeling dough and mold into shapes.

Ice Cream

1 can Eagle brand milk

2 3-oz. boxes instant pudding and pie mix (any flavor)
Mix all the above ingredients with 3 cups whole milk. Pour into churn and finish with milk. Makes 4 quarts and takes about 20–25 minutes to freeze.

Sugar Cookies

1/2 cup butter
1 egg
2 1/2 cups flour
1 teaspoon baking powder
1/4 teaspoon salt
1 cup sugar
1/2 teaspoon flavoring, lemon or vanilla
Cream butter, sugar and egg together. Add dry ingredients. Knead and chill overnight (for best results). Roll and cut 1/4 inch thick. Cut with cookie cutter or jar lid. Bake at 350 degrees until brown. You may eat plain or frost them.

Birthday Cake

1 box Duncan Hines Butter Cake Mix
3 eggs
1/2 cup butter
2/3 cup water
Mix all the above ingredients with mixer for 2–3 minutes. Pour into greased tube pan and bake according to time listed on back of box.

Peanut Brittle

2 cups raw peanuts
1/2 cup Karo syrup
1/4 cup water
1 teaspoon baking soda
Mix nuts, syrup, water, and sugar in pot.
Cook on high heat, stirring constantly for approximately 6–8 minutes.
Drop some of the mixture in cold water. If it hardens, remove from stove.
Stir in baking soda and pour on aluminum foil, let cool.
Break into small pieces, eat and enjoy.

Spice Drop Cookies

1 package spice cake mix
1/2 cup apple sauce

1/2 cup salad oil
1 egg
1/4 cup raisins
1/4 cup chopped nuts (optional)

Mix together cake mix, apple sauce, salad oil, and egg. Beat with electric mixer until smooth. Mix raisins and nuts. Cover and place in refrigerator for several hours. Spoon by teaspoonfuls onto cookie sheet. Bake at 350 degrees for 15 minutes.

Makes about 3 dozen cookies.

Peanut Butter Balls

1 cup graham cracker crumbs
2 sticks butter
1 box powdered sugar
1/2 cup peanut butter (crunchy)
1/2 cup nuts
1 teaspoon vanilla

Knead together, form into small balls.

Melt 1 cup semi-sweet chocolate bits in 1/2 cake of paraffin. Dip balls in chocolate, place on a greased surface, let cool.

Let your child help with the recipes and measuring of the ingredients. Talk about color, taste, texture and shape. Have fun and enjoy these recipes.

FALL INTO SPRING ACTIVITIES
(Ages Four to Twelve)

Calendar

Month-To-Month

September

Saturday

Go with child to a mall, mull around; compare window decorations; sit in on concerts; explore exhibits.

Sunday

- Go to church or other place of worship.
- Go to a park.
- Read newspaper to find free and inexpensive entertainment.
- Do something special for a sibling (brother or sister).

My accomplishments for September _____

October

- Plan a *neighborhood* party at home. Children and parents exchange dress (parents as kids, kids as parents). Serve apples, cider, popcorn.
- Learn something about another ethnic or national group during United Nations month.
- Go to a football game (or other athletic events).
- Watch a TV movie together.
- Go to church or other place of worship.

My accomplishments for October _____

November

- Plan a fall picnic in a park (hot dog, hot chocolate, etc.).
- Take a neighborhood friend along.
- Look for acorns, pine cones, leaves—colors and shapes.
- Go to church or other place of worship.
- Celebrate Thanksgiving by doing a good deed.
- Watch PBS (Public Broadcasting Service) for at least an hour a week.
- Go to a football game or other winter sports.

My accomplishments for November _____

December

- Make at least one gift.
- *Give a gift* of a story hour at a nursery; read to elderly patients at a nursing home.
- Parent and child make cookies together.
- Go shopping together (parent/child/sibling/friends).
- Use vacation time to read a book; write a letter, visit.
- Observe Kwanza (December 26) or other ethnic holiday.

My accomplishments for December _____

January

- Go to church or other place of worship.
- Check out a book from the library on an issue.
- Go to a flea market.
- Watch PBS for at least one hour a week.
- Observe Emancipation Day (January 1).
- Work on family photo album.

My accomplishments for January _____

February

- Make paper valentines.
- Decorate home or room with hearts.
- Invite friends in for *oldies* but *goodies* love songs; have parents tell about their courtship.
- Make valentine cookies; take a batch to a nursing home.
- Buy an African-American book, picture, or articles of clothing.
- Attend two black history events.
- Learn about at least one African-American (or other ethnic) personality.
- Learn more about your family.
- Go to church or other place of worship.

My accomplishments for February _____

March

- Start a *window seal* garden.
- Go to a free lecture.
- Go to church or other place of worship.
- Read a book; begin a reading diary.
- See a play (concert, etc.).
- Do something for a sibling or friend.

My accomplishments for March _____

April

- Decorate home, yard and/or room for Easter.
- Have an Easter egg hunt.
- Plan a spring outdoor activity.
- Clean out closet.
- Paint something around the house.
- Go to church or other place of worship.

My accomplishments for April _____

May

- Collect names and addresses of friends who may be moving.
- Participate in school closing activities.
- Volunteer with a *spring cleanup* project.
- Start planning for vacation time.
- Plan meaningful as well as fun things.

- Set goal(s) for summer (learn to swim, paint, drive, garden, learn more about a subject, practice health habits, work and save, etc.).
- Serve mother breakfast in bed.
- Make or purchase gift for mom.
- Go to church or other place of worship.

My accomplishments for May _____

June

See the excerpts from the *Summer Sharing Book* (a booklet of activities for parent/younger child sharing).

Caring-Sharing Together Activities

Four- to Five-Year-Olds
Pre-School — Kindergarten
Day-To-Day — Any Day

At Home

- Teach child how to use the telephone book.
- Teach child how to use a measuring cup.
- Teach child how to use a calendar.
- Teach child how to read a clock.
- Teach child how to read a scale.
- Let child examine shapes; lids and curves, boxes and bags; tall-short; round, square.
- Let child fold dinner napkins into different shapes: squares, oblongs, triangles.
- Let child count petals on a flower.
- READ to child from a book at least once a day.

All Around

- Take a listening walk together. Hear the _____; point out sounds. Examine a dew drop on a leaf.
- Read labels on boxes at the grocery store and at home.
- Show child the contents and weights written on packages at grocery store.
- Let child find items.

Some Major Learnings At This Stage

Reading	Cooperating	Writing
Sharing	Computing	Self-Confidence

Six-Year-Olds—Grade I
Day-To-Day—Any Day

At Home

- Provide place (corner, etc.) that is well lighted for *homework* sessions.
- Draw floor plan of the house and measure.
- Perfect *telling time.*
- Set the table for meals.
- Pronounce words child cannot. Introduce new words parenthetically (ex. *ordeal* [very difficult, hard to do, trying]).
- Write letters parent to child, child to parent.
- Let child take care of: (a) plant, (b) pet, (c) others.
- Have child look at newspaper.
- Read relevant news items and explain.

All Around

- Have child tell prices of items at grocery store.
- Take child to post office.
- Note surroundings when going driving.
- Point out differences in buildings, plants, landscape.

Some Major Learnings At This Stage

Writing	Comparing	Social Concepts
Responsibilities (caring for)		

Seven-Year-Olds—Grade II
Day-To-Day—Any Day

At Home

- Make flash cards to help with addition and subtraction.
- Start morning on high note with conversation.
- Make up words from brand names on boxes, containers.
- Make list of chores and keep a checklist of those completed.
- Talk to child at beginning and end of day about plans and experiences.

All Around

- Collect restaurant menus and read them.
- Estimate costs of items at the store.
- Car games: find letters-alphabets on car license plates.
- Keep a list of states seen on license tags and/or visited.
- Note state logos (symbols) on license plates.

Some Major Learnings At This Stage

Alphabetize	Reading Comprehension
Calculate	Classify
Cooperate	Differentiate

Eight-Year-Olds—Grade III
Day-To-Day—Any Day

At Home

- Discuss books child reads during the day.
- Let child help plan dinner.
- Discuss child's allowance.
- Have child complete daily household task.
- Put child in charge of recycles, etc.
- Have child get mail from box and sort it by types: statements, advertising, personal letters, etc.
- Let child watch you write a check.
- Help child use dictionary.

All Around

- Have child examine grocery bill; match items with receipt.
- Have child ask for the clothes that are picked up at the dry cleaners.
- Let child discuss change from bills.

Some Major Learnings At This Stage

How to study	Homework
Paired learning	Expressing ideas

Nine-Year-Olds—Grade IV
Day-To-Day—Any Day

At Home

- Have child learn to read bus and train schedules.
- Examine maps and choose routes to (a) church, (b) parent work site(s), (c) etc.

- Have tool box and equip it with measuring instruments.
- Ask child about day's learnings and activities at school.
- Help child broaden vocabulary with a word game.
- Read current events from local newspaper.

All Around

- When shopping, have child compare brand names.
- Open a savings account for child; let him/her use own money.
- Visit someone in need and have child undertake a chore for that person.
- Take child with you to a government building.
- Take child with you to voting place.
- Read building directories.

Some Major Learnings At This Stage

Simple research procedure
Beginning to learn meanings of metaphors and imagery
Structure of government (local, state, federal)

Ten-Year-Olds—Grade V
Day-To-Day—Any Day

At Home

- Stress values to your child.
- Keep track of child's friends.
- Note your feelings tactfully.
- Supervise videos, late shows, R-rated films.
- Help child in homework when you know the material.
- Find topics for dinner conversation.
- Write a story (turn off TV and imagine).
- Discourage preoccupation with fads, bizarre hair-dos, expensive clothes and gadgets.

All Around

- Go to a movie together
- Visit the library together.
- Visit a museum together.
- Go to an auction—learn about pricings of old things.
- When shopping, have child compare ounce to ounce and pound to pound versus price.
- Take notes on trips.
- Observe phenomena in environment.

Some Major Learnings At This Stage

Self-worth   Peer associations   Friends
Decision making

Eleven-Year-Olds—Grade VI
Day-To-Day—Any Day

At Home

- Household and homework chores should be undertaken and completed.
- Allow for freedom of expression.
- Teach child how to handle emergencies at home (turn off water, shut off electric power, call ambulance, fire and police departments).
- Discuss occupations.
- Let child handle grocery budget for a month.
- Play investment games at home.
- Have discussions on the workings of the human body.

All Around

- Occasionally, for a brief visit, take your child to work with you. Let child see that work is meaningful. (Do not let child be disruptive.)
- Take child to public meetings of local affairs (city council, public hearings).
- Take child to a musical, a play, or other concerts.
- Let child volunteer to work with a political party of choice.

Some Major Learnings At This Stage

Academic demands	Do's and don'ts in society
Public affairs	Managing mood changes
Citizenship responsibility	Present personal opinions in effective manner

Twelve-Year-Olds—Grade VII
Day-To-Day—Any Day

At Home

- Give child safe outlet for venting anger.
- Make sure child has you or a special adult to talk to when upset.
- Encourage child to read *about* issues and subjects.
- Make news items a part of daily conversations.
- Use humor whenever possible to relieve family stress.

All Around
- Join the local Y; take extracurricular classes.
- Join a social club at school, church.
- Decide on age to send child off to the store by him or herself.

Some Major Learnings At This Stage

Life realities   Rationale of rules
Adapting to change   Critical thinking
Broader view of self in relation to others

Making the Grade

How to ensure that your child will succeed in school:

1. Promote Respect
2. Teach Responsibility
3. Encourage Resourcefulness
   Enrichment experiences help **but** without these three R's little else
   works:

RESPECT
RESPONSIBILITY
RESOURCEFULNESS

CHILDREN LEARN
WHAT THEY LIVE

If a child lives with criticism, He learns to condemn.

If a child lives with hostility, He learns to fight.

If a child lives with ridicule, He learns to be shy.

If a child lives with shame, He learns to feel guilty.

If a child lives with encouragement, He learns confidence.

If a child lives with praise, He learns to appreciate.

If a child lives with security, He learns to have faith.

If a child lives with approval, He learns to like himself.

If a child lives with acceptance and friendship,

He learns to find love in the world.

Dorthy Law Nolte

REFERENCES

Abbott, J. C., & Sabatina, D. A. (1975). Teacher-mom intervention with academic high-risk preschool children. *Exceptional Children, 41*(4), 267–68.

Atkins, Janet, et al. (1988). *Listening to parents. An approach to improvement of home/school relations.* London: Croom Helm.

Boskin, Martin (1975). *Parent power. A candid handbook for dealing with your child's school.* New York: Walker.

Collins, C. H. (1982). *The home school connection: Selected partnership programs in large cities.* Boston: Institute for Responsive Education.

Comer, J. P., & Poussiant, A. (1992). *Raising black children.* New York: Penguin USA.

Cruz, N. et al. (1981). *A catalog of parent involvement projects: A collection of quality parent projects for assisting children in the achievement of basic skills.* Rosslyn, VA: Inter-American Research Associates.

Edwards, P., & Young, L. (1992, September). Beyond parents: family, community and school involvement. *Phi Delta Kappan, 74,* 72+.

Effective schools for children-at-risk (video) 25 minutes. 42-page leaders' guide. Association for Supervision and Curriculum Development.

Fontana, V., & Moolman, V. (1991). *Save the family. Save the child. What can we do to help children at risk?* New York: Penguin USA.

Golden, L., & Capuzzi, D. (1986). *Helping families help children: Family interventions with school related problems.* Springfield, IL: Charles C Thomas, Publisher.

Gordon, I. J. (1969). Developing parent power. In E. Grothberg (Ed.), *Critical issues in research related to disadvantaged children.* Princeton, NJ: Educational Testing Service.

Guidelines for Parent-Teacher Conferences (Video) 28 minutes, with Leader's Manual and Eager to Learn Book. Association for Supervision and Curriculum Development.

Little things make a big difference (video) 16 minutes; col. National Association of Elementary School Principals and World Book Educational Products.

Lombana, J. H. (1983). *Home-school partnerships: Guidelines for educators.* New York: Grune and Stratton.

Losen, S. M. et al. (1978). *Parent conferences in the schools. Procedures for developing effective partnerships.* Boston: Allyn and Bacon.

McCallon, E., & McCray (1975). *Planning and conducting interviews.* Austin, TX: Learning Concepts.

McLoughlin, C. S. (1987). *Parent teacher conferencing.* Springfield, IL: Charles C Thomas, Publisher.

Morrison, G. S. (1978). *Parent involvement in the home, school, and community.* Columbus, OH: Charles E. Merrill.

Morton-Young, T. (1992). *Summer Sharing Book. Activities for the younger child.* Greensboro, NC: NAACP Special Project.

——. (1976). Parent practica, in *Start early for an early start.* Chicago: ALA.

Rich, D. (1985). *The forgotten factor in school success: The family. A policymaker's guide.* Washington, DC: Home and Schools Institute.

Rutherford, R. B., Jr., & Edgar, E. (1979). *Teachers and parents. A guide to intervention cooperation.* Boston: Allyn and Bacon.

Samuda, R. (Ed.), & Shies, K. (1986). *Multicultural education programs and methods.* Toronto: Intercultural Social Sciences Publications, Inc.

United States Department of Health and Human Services, Public Health Service. (1991). *Parent training is prevention . . .* DHHS Publication No. (ADM) 91-1715. Washington, DC: Government Printing Office.

Wardlaw, H., & Bye, T. (1990, January). Parent education reflects community partnership in Valejo. *Thrust, 19,* 45–47.

Wolfendale, S. (1983). *Parental participation in children's development and education.* London: Gordon and Breach.

PART IV

DIRECTORY OF RESOURCES

Academic Therapy Publications	20 Commercial Boulevard Novato, CA 94949-6191
Addison-Wesley Publishing Company	South Street Reading, MA 01867
Afro-American Publishing Company	1927 S. Indiana Ave. Chicago, IL 60616
American Guidance Service (AGS)	Publishers Bldg. Circle Pines, MN 55014
Argus Communication	7440 Natchez Avenue Niles, IL 60648
B & T Learning Materials	1515 Broadway New York, NY 11510
Bell & Howell Equipment Company	7100 McCormick Rd. Chicago, IL 60645
Black Books Bulletin	7850 S. Ellis Ave. Chicago, IL 60619
Edward W. Blyden Press	P.O. Box 621 Manhattanville P.O. New York, NY 10027
Books for Our Children, Inc.	Dept. P, 513 Manhattan Ave. New York, NY 10027
Borg-Warner Educational Systems	600 W. University Ave. Arlington Heights, IL 60004
Bowmar/Noble Publications	4563 Colorado Blvd. Los Angeles, CA 90039
Milton Bradley	Springfield, MA 01105
Brown Bear Books	P.O. Box 780 D Englewood, NJ 07631

Cassettes Unlimited	Roanoke, TX 76262
Childcraft	20 Kilmer Rd. Edison, NJ 08817
Child Guidance	P.O. Box 113 Bronx, NY 10472
Child's World	P.O. Box 681 Elgin, IL 60120
Classroom Materials Company	93 Myrtle Dr. Great Neck, NY 11021
Children's Press (Division of Regensteiner)	1224 W. Van Buren St. Chicago, IL 60607
Constructive Playthings	P.O. Box 5445 1040 E. 85th St. Kansas City, MO 64131
Continental Press	P.O. Box 554 Elgin, IL 60120
	2336 Farrington St. Dallas, TX 75207
	c/o Vroman's 2085 E. Foothill Blvd. Pasadena, CA 91109
	Elizabethtown, PA 17022
	127 International Blvd., N.W. Atlanta, GA 30303
	407 S.W. 11th Ave. Portland, OR 97205
Coronet Media	65 E. South Water St. Chicago, IL 60601
Creative Playthings (CBS Toys, Div. of CBS)	41 Madison Ave. New York, NY 10010
Creative Teaching Associates	P.O. Box 7766 Fresno, CA 93747
Cuisenaire of America	12 Church St. New Rochelle, NY 10805
Curriculum Associates	5 Esquire Road North Billerica, MA 01862

John Day Company c/o Harper & Row Publications	Distributed by: Harper & Row Keystone Industrial Park Scranton, PA 18512
Demco Educational Corporation	P.O. Box 7488 Madison, WI 53707
Dennison Manufacturing Company	Framingham, MA 01701
Denoyer-Geppert Company	5235 Ravenswood Ave. Chicago, IL 60640
Developmental Learning Materials (DLM)	7440 Natchez Ave. Niles, IL 60648
Disney Educational Media Company	500 W. Buena Vista St. Burbank, CA 91521
Edmark Associates	P.O. Box 3903 Bellevue, WA 98009
Edu/Cards Corp. (Subsidiary of Binney & Smith)	1100 Church Lane P.O. Box 431 Easton, PA 18402
Educational Activities	1937 Grand Ave. Baldwin, NY 11510
Educational Design	47 West 13th St. New York, NY 10011
Educational Development Corporation	P.O. Box 45663 Tulsa, OK 74145
Educational Insights	20435 S. Tillman Ave. Carson, CA 90746

Educational Progress (Division of
  Educational Development
  Corporation)
	P.O. Box 45663
	Tulsa, OK 74145

Educational Projections
  Corporation (Division of
  Standard Projector and
  Equipment Company)
	3070 Lake Terrace
	Glenview, IL 60025

Educational Reading Services	320 Rt. 17 Mahwah, NJ 07430

Educational Record Sales	157 Chambers St. New York, NY 10007
Educational Research Associates	P.O. Box 6604 Philadelphia, PA 19149
	333 S.W. Park Ave. 4th Floor Portland, OR 97205
Educational Teaching Aids (Division of A. Daigger and Company)	159 W. Kinzie St. Chicago, IL 60610
Educators Publishing Service (EPS)	75 Moulton St. Cambridge, MA 02138
Encyclopedia Britannica Educational Corporation	422 N. Michigan Ave. Chicago, IL 60611
Enrichment Reading Corporation of America	Iron Ridge, WI 53035
Enrichment Reading Services	320 Rt. 17 Mahwah, NJ 07430
ESP	1201 E. Johnson P.O. Box 5037 Jonesboro, AR 72401
Exceptional Child Development Center	725 Liberty Ave. Pittsburgh, PA 15222
Eye Gate Media	146-01 Archer Ave. Jamaica, NY 11435
Far West Laboratories Department of Education	P.O. Box 271 Sacramento, CA 95802
Fearon Education Division Pitman Learning	P.O. Box 741 Belmont, CA 94002
Follett Publishing Co. (Division of Follett Corporation)	1010 W. Washington Blvd. Chicago, IL 60607
Gamco Industries (Division of Siboney Corporation)	P.O. Box 310 Big Spring, TX 79720
Garrard Publishing Company	1607 N. Market St. Champaign, IL 61820

Ginn & Company (Division of Xerox)	Education Center P.O. Box 2649 1250 Fairwood Ave. Columbus, OH 43216
Golden Press (Division of Western Publishing Company)	P.O. Box 708 Racine, WI 53401
Great Ideas	40 Oser Ave. Hauppauge, NY 11787
Harper & Row Publishers	10 E. 53rd Street New York, NY 10022
Hayes School Publishing Company	321 Pennwood Ave. Wilkinsburg, PA 15221
Highlights for Children	P.O. Box 269 2300 W. Fifth Ave. Columbus, OH 43216
Holiday Games	P.O. Box 2565 Bell Gardens, CA 90201
Holt, Rinehart & Winston (Division of CBS)	383 Madison Ave. New York, NY 10017
Hoover Brothers	1305 N. 14th St. Temple, TX 76501
Houghton Mifflin Company	One Beacon St. Boston, MA 02107
Hubbard	P.O. Box 104 Northbrook, IL 60453
Ideal School Supply	11000 S. Lavergne Ave. Oak Lawn, IL 60453
Imperial International Learning Corporation	P.O. Box 548 Kankakee, IL 60901
Incentives for Learning	600 W. Van Buren St. Chicago, IL 60607
Instructional Fair	P.O. Box 1650 Grand Rapids, MI 49501
Instructional Materials and Equipment Distributors	1520 Cotner Ave. Los Angeles, CA 90025

Instructo/McGraw-Hill	Cedar Hollow Road Paoli, PA 19301
The Instructor Publications (Division of Harcourt, Brace, Jovanovich)	P.O. Box 6099 Duluth, MN 55806
Interpretive Education (Division of I. E. Products)	2306 Winters Dr. Kalamazoo, MI 49002
Janus Book Publishers	2501 Industrial Parkway, West Hayward, CA 94545
Jayfro Corporation	P.O. Box 400 Waterford, CT 06385
Johnson Publishing Company	820 S. Michigan Ave. Chicago, IL 60605
The Judy Company	250 James St. Morristown, NJ 07960
Kenworthy Educational Service	P.O. Box 60, Dept. E Buffalo, NY 14205
Kid's Stuff/Incentive Publications	2400 Crestmoor Nashville, TN 37215
Kimbo Educational	P.O. Box 477 Long Branch, NJ 07740
Lakeshore Curriculum Materials Center	2695 Dominguez Carson, CA 90749
Learning Arts	P.O. Box 170 Wichita, KS 67201
Learning Concepts	400 E. Anderson Lane Austin, TX 78705
Learning Corporation of America	1350 Avenue of the Americas New York, NY 10019
Learning Discoveries	P.O. Box 23077 10655 S.W. Greenburg Rd. Portland, OR 97223
Learning Research Associates	1501 Broadway New York, NY 10036
Learning Systems Corporation (Division of Richard D. Irwin, Inc.)	1818 Ridge Rd. Homewood, IL 60430

Learning Tree Filmstrips	934 Pearl St. Box 1590, Dept. 525 Boulder, CO 80806
Love Publishing Co.	6635 E. Villanova Place Denver, CO 80222
Macmillan Company	866 Third Avenue New York, NY 10022
	Front and Brown Sts. Riverside, NJ 08075
Mafex Associates	90 Cherry St. P.O. Box 519 Johnstown, PA 15907
Marsh Films Enterprises	P.O. Box 8082 Shawnee Mission, KS 66208
McGraw-Hill Book Company	1221 Avenue of the Americas New York, NY 10020
McGraw-Hill Book Company Ryerson Press	330 Progress Don Mills, Ontario, Canada
McGraw-Hill Films	110 15th St. Del Mar, CA 92104
Media Materials	2936 Remington Ave. Dept. E 98 Baltimore, MD 21211
Charles E. Merrill Publishing Company (Division of Bell & Howell)	1300 Alum Creek Dr. Columbus, OH 43216
Milliken Publishing Company	1100 Research Blvd. St. Louis, MO 63132
Modern Education Corporation	P.O. Box 721 Tulsa, OK 74101
National Association for the Deaf	814 Thayer St. Silver Springs, MD 20910
National Association of School Principals	1615 Duke Street Alexandria, VA 22314
National Textbook Co.	8259 Niles Center Rd. Skokie, IL 60077

New Day Press	2355 E. 89th St. Cleveland, OH 44106
Newspaper Enterprise Association	230 Park Ave. New York, NY 10017
Novo Educational Toy and Equipment Corporation	585 Avenue of the Americas New York, NY 10011
Opportunities for Learning	8950 Lurline Dept. A979 Chatsworth, CA 91311
Perception Development Research Assoc.	P.O. Box 827 Port Angeles, WA 98362
Playskool (Division of Milton Bradley)	Springfield, MA 01101
Prentice-Hall Learning Systems	P.O. Box 527 San Jose, CA 95106
Radiant Educational Corporation	Morton Grove, IL 66053
Random House	400 Hahn Rd. Westminster, MD 21157
Reader's Digest Services	Educational Division Pleasantville, NY 10570
Rhythm Records (A.B. LeCrone)	819 N.W. 92nd St. Oklahoma City, OK 73114
Sapphire Publishing Company	P.O. Box 15072 San Francisco, CA 94115
Frank Schaffer Publications	26616 Indian Peak Road Rancho Palos Verdes, CA 90274
Scholastic Book Services	904 Sylvan Ave. Englewood Cliffs, NJ 07632
Science Research Associates (SRA) (Division of IBM)	155 North Wacker Dr. Chicago, IL 60606
Scott Education Division	Lower Westfield Rd. Holyoke, MA 01040
Scott Foresman & Company	1900 E. Lake Ave. Glenview, IL 60025
Dale Seymour Publications	P.O. Box 10888 Palo Alto, CA 94303

Show & Tell Products	17657 Ridgecreek Rd. Cleveland, OH 44107
L. W. Singer Company	3750 Monroe Ave. Rochester, NY 14603
Society for Visual Education (Subsidiary of the Singer Education Division)	1345 Diversey Parkway Chicago, IL 60614
St. Regis Instructional Materials	3300 Pinson Valley Parkway Birmingham, AL 35217
Steck-Vaughan Company (Division of Intext)	P.O. Box 2028 807 Brazos Austin, TX 78768
Teachers College Press	1234 Amsterdam Ave. New York, NY 10027
Teachers Publishing Corporation	100F Brown St. Riverside, NJ 08075
Teaching Resources Corporation	50 Pond Park Road Hingham, MA 02043
Texas Instruments	13500 N. Central Expressway P.O. Box 5012, M/S 54 Dallas, TX 75222
3M Company	General Office 3M Center St. Paul, MN 55101
Third World Press	7524 S. Cottage Grove Ave. Chicago, IL 60619
Trend Enterprises	P.O. Box 43073 St. Paul, MN 55164
Troll Associates	320 Rt. 17 Mahwah, NJ 07430
United Learning	6633 W. Howard St. Niles, IL 60648
United States Government Printing Office	Division of Public Documents Washington, DC 20360
Valient Instructional Materials Corporation	195 Bonhomme St. Hackensack, NJ 07062

Vanguard Visuals Corporation	P.O. Box 24266 Dallas, TX 75224
Weber Costello	1900 N. Narragansett Avenue Chicago, IL 60639
Webster Division (Division or McGraw-Hill)	1221 Avenue of the Americas New York, NY 10020
Western Publishing Company	1220 Mound Avenue Racine, WI 53401
Chandler White Publishing Company	30 E. Huron St., Suite 4403 Chicago, IL 60611
Wilson Educational Media (Division of H. Wilson Corporation)	555 W. Taft Drive South Holland, IL 60473
Wise Owl Publications	P.O. Box 3816 Los Angeles, CA 90028
Wonder Books (Division of Grosset & Dunlap)	51 Madison Avenue New York, NY 10010
World Book—Childcraft International (A subsidiary of the Scott-Fetzer Company)	Merchandise Mart Plaza Chicago, IL 60654
World Book Educational Products Station 9/NAESP	101 North West Point Blvd. Elk Grove Village, IL 60007
Xerox Education Publications	P.O. Box 2639 1250 Fairwood Avenue Columbus, OH 43216

PERIODICALS AND MISCELLANEOUS

AIDS FOR EDUCATION. CD Publications
8204 Fenton St., 2nd Fl.
Silver Springs, MD 20190-4509.
Public and private funding opportunities for all levels of education.

AMERICAN FAMILY
1221 Massachusetts Ave., N.W., #B,
Washington, DC 20005-5302.
Monitors societal and family changes with emphasis on young marrieds and single parents and their future.

**BETTER TEACHING TIPS: TIPS AND TECHNIQUES TO IM-
PROVE STUDENT LEARNING.** National School Public Relations
Association.
1501 Lee Highway, #201
Arlington, VA 22209-1109

BLACK STUDENT ADVISOR. Beckham House Publishers, Inc.
2 Eaton St., #814
Hampton, VA 23669

CENTER FOR PARENT EDUCATION NEWSLETTER
Center for Parent Education.
81 Wyman St.
Waltham, MA 02160

CHILD. New York Times Magazine Group
110 5th Ave.
New York, NY 10011-5601
 Edited for parents of elementary school children.

CURRICULUM (C.A.S.) Curriculum Advisory Service.
407 S. Dearborn St., #1360
Chicago, IL 60605-1111

FAMILY JOURNAL. W.J. Wheeler Publishing, Inc.
R.D. 2, P.O. Box 165
Putney, VT 05346

FAMILY MAGAZINE. Minority Press Association.
5121 Parallel Parkway, #9
Kansas City, KS 66104-3165
 Focus is on the African-American family.

FAMILY RESOURCE COALITION REPORT. Family Resource Coalition.
230 N. Michigan Ave., #1625
Chicago, IL 60601-5910
 Public school education focus for parents raising children.

LEADER. Active Parenting Publishers
810-D Franklin Ct., #8
Marietta, GA 30067-8939
 Video-based parent education programs.

LEARNING. Education Today, Inc.
530 University Ave.
Palo Alto, CA 94301

PARENT HOTLINE. Child Growth and Development Corporation.
599 Broadway, 9th Fl.
New York, NY 10012
SPEAK OUT FOR CHILDREN. National Council for Children's Rights
220 I Street, NW, Suite 230
Washington, DC 20000-4307
   Strengthening families and assisting children of separation and
   divorce.

STEPFAMILIES AND BEYOND (Stepparent News). Listening, Inc.
8716 Pine Ave.
Gary, IN 46403-1411

OTHER RESOURCES

Agencies

Action for Children's Television
46 Austin Street
Newtonville, MA 02160

Administration for Children, Youth and Families
Office of Human Development Services
Department of Health and Human Services
200 Independence Ave., SW
Washington, DC 20201

Associates for Troubled Children
19730 Ventura Blvd., Suite 1A
Woodland Hills, CA 91364

Association for Childhood Education International
11141 Georgia Ave., Suite 200
Wheaton, MD 20902

Big Brothers/Big Sisters of America
117 South 17th St., Suite 1200
Philadelphia, PA 19103

Black Parenting: Relevant Educational Corporation, Inc.
4465 S. 4th St.
Arlington, VA

Center for Organizational and Community Development
School of Education, Room 225
University of Massachusetts
Amherst, MA 01003

Child Welfare League of America (CWLA)
67 Irving Place
New York, NY 10003

Children's Defense Fund
1520 New Hampshire Ave., NW
Washington, DC 20005

Council for Exceptional Children
1920 Association Drive
Reston, VA 22091

Family Resource Coalition
230 N. Michigan Ave., Suite 1625
Chicago, IL 60601

Family Support Center
2 Baily Road
Yeadon, PA 19050

Foster Grandparents
808 Connecticut Ave., NW
Washington, DC 20525

High/Scope Educational Research Foundation
Family Programs Department
600 River Street
Ypsilanti, MI 48197

Los Niños Bien Educados (for Hispanic parents. See Center for Improvement of Child Caring under "Parent Programs".)

National Alliance of Black School Educators
2816 Georgia Ave., NW
Washington, DC 20001

National Alliance Concerned with Teenage Parents
7315 Wisconsin Ave.
Washington, DC 20014

National Association of Homes for Children
104 E. 35th Street
New York, NY 10016

National Association of Neighbors
1651 Fuller, NW
Washington, DC 20009

National Association of Secondary School Principals
1904 Association Drive
Reston, VA 22091

National Black Child Development Institute, Inc.
1023 15th St., NW, Suite 600
Washington, DC 20005

National Committee for Citizens in Education
Little Patuxent Parkway, Suite 301
Columbia, MD 21044

National Congress of Parents and Teachers (PTA)
700 N. Rush Street
Chicago, IL 60601

National Education Association
1200 16th St., NW
Washington, DC 20036

National Hispanic Families
1511 K Street, NW, Suite 1026
Washington, DC 20005

National School Volunteer Program, Inc.
701 N. Fairfax Street, Suite 320
Alexandria, VA 22314

Northwest Indian Child Welfare Institute
Parry Center for Children
3415 S.E. Powell Blvd.
Portland, OR 97202

Parenting Materials Information Center
Southwest Educational Development Laboratory
211 E. Seventh Street
Austin, TX 78701

Parents Without Partners
8807 Colesville Rd.
Silver Spring, MD 20910

The Youth Project
2355 18th Street, NW
Washington, DC 20009

INDEX